# TEENAGER IN A DRUGGED SOCIETY
## A SYMPTOM OF CRISIS

# THE TEENAGER IN A DRUGGED SOCIETY

## A Symptom of Crisis

by CELIA SPALTER DESCHIN, Ph.D.

*Man is on earth not merely to be happy but to realize great things.*

Vincent van Gogh in a letter to his brother Theo.

*Standard Book Number:* 8239–0226–9
*Library of Congress Catalog Card Number:* 72–190581

Published in 1972 by Richards Rosen Press, Inc.
29 East 21st Street, New York City, N.Y. 10010

*First Edition*

*Manufactured in the United States of America*

## About the Author

Celia Spalter Deschin's educational and professional background reflects significant changes in American life from World War I to the present. She obtained an A.B. degree *cum laude* from Smith College in 1924 and was elected to Phi Beta Kappa. For some years thereafter she followed a teaching career. Becoming interested in social work, in 1942 she obtained an M.S. from the Columbia University School of Social Work. After gaining wide experience in that field, she became a doctoral candidate, and in 1958 New York University granted her a PH.D. degree with an award for "outstanding scholarship."

Since then Dr. Deschin has followed a career of teaching, writing, and research, as well as engaging in a variety of professional and community activities. Her study *Teen-Agers and Venereal Disease* attracted international attention and led her to write the book *The Teenager and VD: A Social Symptom of Our Times* (1969). In 1961 she became Professor of Research at the Adelphi University School of Social Work, and in 1968 she was appointed Professor Emeritus. Her wide-ranging research projects include a study of delinquency in Nassau County, New York, and *A Community Self-Portrait,* which emphasized values, patterns of child-rearing, and intergroup relations in suburbia. In 1971 she completed a study of the effects of integration of orthopedically handicapped children with nonhandicapped peers.

Since 1966 Dr. Deschin has been involved in a program of drug treatment and rehabilitation in Nassau County and has been an active member of the Nassau County Drug Abuse and Addiction Commission. She is a frequent contributor to professional publications and has appeared as a lecturer on radio and television. Her professional affiliations include membership in the American Association for the Advancement of Science, American Sociological Association, and the National Association of Social Workers; and Fellowship in the American Orthopsychiatric Association, the Society for the Scientific Study of Sex, and the American Public Health Association. She is listed in "Who's Who of American Women."

# Acknowledgments

It is not possible to write about drug abuse and addiction in the 1970's without involving more people than it is possible to thank individually. Among them were those who listened patiently as I thought out loud; others were students, drug users and non-users alike, who willingly shared their experience and knowledge of drug use.

They talked with me freely, without restraint, in the confidence, I believe, that I would write about the subject honestly and with their concern in mind, even when they were aware that my views might well be radically different from theirs, in particular on the point that it is necessary to try drugs, at the very least, before one can gain an understanding of them. To all of these young people who gave of their time and confidence, I owe a special debt of gratitude.

To Seymour Rudner, Director of Research and Evaluation on the staff of the Nassau County Drug Abuse and Addiction Commission, my appreciation for his readiness to share his knowledge of drug abuse and addiction even before I became involved in writing the book, as well as for his helpful support throughout the difficult period of collecting data and other preparation. His help was all the more valuable because of the widespread confusion, disagreement, and misunderstanding that persist even among authorities and professionals in the field. I am thankful in particular for his help with Chapter VI, which deals with the description and classification of the drugs in general use by adolescents, and for his careful reading of the completed manuscript.

To Helen Brooks, a dear friend, and to my husband, Jacob Deschin, I owe more than I can adequately express. The loss of a typist with whom I had worked for years, together with the need to comprehend the problem as fully as possible *before* I could begin the writing, meant that I was under tremendous pressure when I began actually to write. Without their support and encouragement, especially during the rough periods when I often despaired of completing the book on time, it is doubtful I could have had the will and the energy necessary for the writing—and, yes, frequent rewriting.

Helen Brooks became an almost constant colleague during the most stressful period, giving unsparingly of her dedicated assistance to assembling material from unusual sources essential for the documentation of what is still a minority view regarding solutions to the drug problem, and for her willingness to share and discuss her understanding of the drug problem as a means of clarifying my views, and I believe hers as well. Far too many books about drugs, I thought—and still do—leave the reader in doubt as to what are really the views of the authors. This is a serious omission, particularly when the problem is as controversial as this one, and the available knowledge so incomplete.

To my husband, I am grateful not only for his cooperation in working night after night, and often into the dawn, typing and editing the manuscript in order to meet the publisher's numerous extended deadlines, this at a time when pressures of his own work were at a maximum, but especially for his belief in the significance of what I was doing.

Celia S. Deschin, Ph.D.
March, 1972

# Contents

# Foreword

In many respects this has been a difficult book to write. The original objective was to provide the kind of information about drugs that would both inform and stimulate adolescents to view drug abuse as a denigration of human potential that could result in lessening the control every human being needs to have over his functioning. Only thus can one learn to solve problems and overcome obstacles, with the help of other human beings rather than by chemical substances. This objective had to be greatly extended. When, for example, it became apparent that nearly pure heroin was becoming readily available to our GI's in Vietnam, I was convinced that the source must be close at hand and set out to ascertain whether this was so. To my amazement, this search led to evidence that our Administration, the Central Intelligence Agency and, of course, the Pentagon were implicated in ways I had not realized. Whether previous Administrations that supported the war in Southeast Asia were similarly involved would require additional research beyond the scope of the present book.

Early in the preparation it was clear that while drug abuse and addiction were seen as symptoms of much that needs improving and changing in American life, too much emphasis continued to be focused on the symptom rather than on the social roots. Hence this part of the book had to be expanded, along with a sharper differentiation between the drug abuse and addiction of youths in our ghettos and the abuse of drugs in affluent neighborhoods and suburbs. In addition, during the necessary field work, in particular, in talking to both adults and adolescents as well as participating in seminars, panel discussions and rap sessions with both drug and nondrug users, I became aware of the importance of dispelling many of the myths that continue to obscure and prevent *more* and *more* effective treatment and rehabilitation programs with built-in evaluation. One myth in particular, needs to be mentioned, namely, that availability plays only a minor role in the spread of drug use, abuse and addiction. The availability that is so largely responsible for the "epidemic" now

9

affecting younger and younger age groups, is supported by widespread social acceptance of drugs to solve personal and social strains and problems. What seemed at the outset to be a predominantly adolescent problem turned out to be an adult problem as well which the young were imitating, but with an intensity that made it appear to have originated with them.

Moreover, while the illegal traffic in heroin for astronomical profits is shocking, no less so is the legal distribution and sale of highly dangerous drugs, many inadequately researched for human use, and again for profits. These drugs become widely available through renewal of prescriptions, as well as through an overproduction far beyond known medical needs, that finds its way into the illicit market and into the hands of elementary, high school and college students. I should add here that when such words as "student," "youth," or "adolescent" are used in the book, what is implied is a proportion of this age grouping. In the absence of reliable statistics regarding youthful drug abuse, it is my observation, based on study of the drug abuse field since 1966 and two and a half years in the preparation of the book, that a majority of today's youth are *not* drug abusers, the mass media and many drug experts to the contrary notwithstanding. It may seem that a majority are on drugs because of the increase in these age groups since the end of World War II.

On all aspects of the drug problems dealt with in the book—even the controversial one of legalization of marijuana—I have not hesitated to take a stand and give my reasons, leaving it to the reader to form his own opinion. And, finally, the book is focused from beginning to end on various ways to prevent new abusers and addicts, and to help those already thus entrapped. No one can say that addicts or drug abusers are beyond cure when no treatment resources are available to them. It is hoped that the book will help readers to answer the questions: What kind of society is it that stimulates individuals, adults and adolescents, to rely on drugs to accomplish that which human beings are preeminently capable of achieving without them, and what must be done to change this?

Celia S. Deschin
Great Neck, N.Y.
March 1972

CHAPTER I

# Are Drugs the Real Problem?

I dedicate this book to the memory of Walter Vandermeer, who died on December 14, 1969, two weeks before his twelfth birthday—"the youngest person ever to be reported dead of an overdose of heroin"—a victim of the kind of society the United States has become. His death, attributed to an overdose of heroin, was accurately diagnosed—but only in biological terms. Stated in human terms, the real cause must be laid to callous indifference and gross neglect on the part of our Administrations—past and present—and their failure to provide adequate funds to solve our major social problems —racism, poverty, unemployment—and to end the war in Vietnam.

Long before his body had been discovered in the "common bathroom of a Harlem tenement," several leading New York City social service agencies, most of them under public auspices, had identified him as "a child in desperate need of care." By the time of his death, "they had exhausted their routine procedures." A school official commented, "There are thousands of Walter Vandermeers out there," and a Family Court judge added, "At least we knew about this one." During his last fourteen months he was left to himself, with no consistent supervision or counseling of any kind, but still searching for adults he could confide in and trust. A month before his death, he looked up John Schoonbeck, a counselor from Patterson House, with whom he had established a warm relationship, only to find that Schoonbeck had left the agency in discouragement and was about to leave the country.[1]

What is hard to accept is the failure of the social agencies to translate their understanding of Walter into appropriate action to help him. Such failure occurs partly through a fragmentation of social services in the name of specialization; partly, as a result of long-standing inadequate funding and staffing of social services in urban ghettos. But to a great extent, it is a national problem arising out of an erosion of our humanity as Americans: not knowing and not caring to know what happens to *all* children.

About the same time that saw the death of Walter Vandermeer,

Walter A. Gilchriest, a 20-year-old student in social studies at the State University of New York at New Paltz, N.Y., "leaped four floors to his death from the roof of a Greenwich Village brownstone." He had been visiting his sister during the holidays. Before he died, he identified himself to the police, saying that he had "leaped under the influence of lysergic acid diethylamide, known as LSD." He was described by the director of the Student Union, where he worked, as a "highly responsible worker and a good student." He was employed in a variety of jobs in order to help pay his way through college, according to Robert D. McFadden's report in *The New York Times* of December 30, 1969. Readers will recall the similar tragic death from LSD of Diane Linkletter, daughter of television personality Art Linkletter, in Los Angeles on October 4, 1969, the result of "a bad trip" on LSD.

Evidence continues to mount that middle-class youngsters are using, singly and in combination, LSD, amphetamines, and barbiturates, all of which are known to be dangerous. In addition, barbiturates are addictive; withdrawal from them is hazardous according to some authorities, even more so than from heroin, requiring medical supervision.

Some idea of the experimentation by adolescents that goes undetected until someone dies may be gained from the report from Pittsburgh (the *New York Post,* July 22, 1970) : "Two teenagers were dead today from an overdose of a drug used in hospitals to relieve the pain of terminal cancer patients. Two other young men and a teenage girl were hospitalized for effects of the same drug."

Since the drug is not bought on the street as is heroin, authorities suggested that the drug probably had been stolen or purchased with a forged prescription. Some of the youths hospitalized were found wandering in a dazed condition in a middle-income area, where it was reported "unofficially" that all five had been at a "get-together."

## Is Heroin on the Rise Among Middle-Class Youth?

Rumors and reports of increasing availability of heroin in high schools and on college campuses in urban centers have given rise to concern that there might be heroin use among middle-class youth. Robert Reinhold, a reporter for *The New York Times,* made a survey of key cities throughout the nation, which was published in the issue of January 12, 1971, under the heading, "Teen-Age Use of Heroin Rising But Data Are Few." Here are excerpts from the report in which he makes clear that the citations are chiefly "anecdotal." In Baltimore,

> Gary, a handsome, clean-cut-looking 18-year-old, the son of a businessman . . . has been "firing" five bags of heroin a day for most

of the last six months. "It's out of control," he says, "You just travel around town and see all these different scenes where people are doing dope."

A 15-year-old girl recently sought treatment at Johns Hopkins Hospital after two years on heroin.

In Pittsburgh,

A 16-year-old boy gets $40 a day from his parents to support his habit, and a 10-year-old addict is under treatment.

In Brooklyn, N.Y.,

An 11-year-old boy was arrested recently on charges of peddling heroin.

In San Francisco,

Reports from San Francisco give no consistent pattern. Health officials feel the number of youngsters "breaking the needle barrier" is rising at a striking rate, but that the situation is far from epidemic. One official estimate is 5 percent of San Francisco's high-school children have tried it, but are not necessarily addicted to it.

In Boston,

Boston is comparable to San Francisco but "about a year behind," said Rev. Richard A. Paine, director of Project PLACE, a social service agency.

The reporter raises the question whether there is evidence of "a growing national epidemic, paralleling that in New York, of heroin addiction among high school age youngsters—not only in the black slums but in the affluent white suburbs." On the basis of conversations with "young heroin addicts, medical men, parents, educators, police and government officials throughout the country," the reporter concludes that the picture is "confused and contradictory. While there is little doubt that use by young people of heroin . . . is rising steadily in some areas of the country and among certain groups, it probably has not reached the epidemic proportions that some have suggested." The reporter cites a federal drug expert (not named) that "heroin abuse is definitely increasing among the young and invading areas it has not before," but, he adds, "this is hard to document—we have only anecdotal evidence."[2]

In Chicago, which is said to "have more heroin addicts than any place except New York and Los Angeles," Dr. Jerome Jaffe, then Director of the State Drug Abuse Program in Illinois, warned: "It

usually hits either the East or West Coast first and then the Midwest
—I think we should be cautious." Dr. Jaffe was subsequently appointed Director of the Special Action Office for Drug Abuse Prevention by Executive Order of June 17, 1971.

## Dissent Among the Experts

Dr. Leon Wurmser, a psychiatrist who heads the Drug Abuse Center
at Johns Hopkins expresses this view:

> Certainly, from all I have seen, it is a fantastic problem—we have
> seen a very substantial number . . . But beyond availability, many
> psychiatrists and sociologists connect heroin use to deep-seated fam-
> ily problems and alienation among middle-class youngsters, and to
> the pressures of group behavior.

His opinion is contradicted by Frank Traynor, assistant to the
superintendent of the Baltimore schools, who states he has not seen
"use of drugs to a serious extent," adding, "I have a great deal of
skepticism that there is a lot of hard stuff. I want to see more before
accepting what appear to be exaggerations."

The *Times* reporter notes that "the difference between the two
men's views reflects the prevailing confusion and misunderstanding
of youthful drug addiction. No one can say how prevalent it is—
*there are no national or local statistics of any real significance.*"
(Italics added.)[3]

Nor is it likely that we will have "national or local statistics" unless
we recognize drug addiction as a sociomedical and public health problem rather than a criminal problem subject to law enforcement control. Viewed thus, heroin addicts, including those who are pushers to
support their own habit, would be considered patients to be treated
by physicians in centers in which an array of treatment and rehabilitative services would be available.

## How Explain Heroin Use Among Middle-class Youth?

The question arises as to how do affluent white youths become involved in heroin use. There are some who say they go the route of
"kicks": from marijuana to pills to heroin. Others say that this occurs through a kind of confused identification with blacks. Heroin
use is a source of profound puzzlement to parents, educators, and
doctors, particularly in middle-class areas, where youngsters were
always considered "too smart" to get hooked by heroin. One explanation, which I have heard over and over again, attributes the beginning
of heroin use to the crackdown on marijuana by Federal authorities

about a year ago—Operation Intercept. This has always seemed to me to be a rationalization rather than an explanation. At best it suggests that marijuana may be psychologically addictive and so a substitute had to be found.

To my knowledge, heroin addiction has occurred largely among those affluent youths who have had few limits set for them. Being able to do what you want when you want to, with no demands made, is productive of tremendous anxiety for an adolescent. Making no demands on such youngsters gives them the impression that they are not needed. That in turn raises doubts as to who they really are, so they try by change and new experiences to search for identity and a place where they *will* be needed. Frequently, these adolescents are unable to make clear they want to be needed. A sensitive adult can sense this and provide guidance and help, but unfortunately not all of today's youngsters in this predicament have been able to find such adults in time.

Some I have known have become involved through failure to solve interpersonal problems with parents, together with school experiences in which no single adult was available to confide in without fear of being reported to the police. But it has been my experience that once away from the ready availability of heroin, together with greater intellectual demands made by college, and with goals more firmly fixed, a number succeed without the intervention of formal treatment to "kick" the habit with the understanding help of non-drug using peers who had initiated 24-hour emergency services, the formation of drug libraries, and had set up services that were educational and therapeutic on a simple but fundamental basis.

The routes to heroin and other dangerous drugs are many. Focus on the drugs or the routes, some of which may have resulted merely by chance at a particular moment in time, is not especially productive. More relevant is a focus on the causal factors that contribute to the use of drugs on the part of adolescents from all walks of life.

Under the headline, "Drug Death of Teen-Ager Shakes an Upstate Town," Michael T. Kaufman of *The New York Times* of August 29, 1970, reported from Hopewell Junction that the community is free of a serious unemployment problem, slums, or even its own police force. It is a "picture of small-town America, a postwar middle-class community." The youth who died was a local Methodist minister's 17-year-old son who had been taking barbiturates and drinking vodka at a party. After the boy's death, it was learned that he had been taken to the hospital twice with drug episodes. Evidence also was found that at least one of the four youths arrested after the death had been picked up on a drug charge before. And in the last year it was reported that "about a dozen kids with overdoses had been picked up."

The worst obstacle, according to detectives, is the "disbelief and hostility that the police receive from parents. This boy's father, on the contrary, wanted his son's death to receive all possible publicity. 'I want people around here to learn a lesson from what has happened'."

Earlier in the year, fourteen youths, including the 18-year-old son of a university chancellor, had been arrested in the South in what state officials characterized as a "major illegal drug operation." The 18-year-old was charged with four counts of possession of narcotics for the purpose of sale. He was held on a $20,000 bond.

## Too Little and Too Late

*The New York Times* of February 17, 1970, reported the death of a 14-year-old boy from an overdose of pills. That occurred "only hours after the Board of Education said it had no funds for security guards to fight the narcotics problem at the school he attended. Three other boys from the same school, Junior High School 52 in the Inwood section of Manhattan, were hospitalized the day before, also apparently from overdoses." The local school board had asked for security guards for all of the schools in the district because parents were becoming increasingly disturbed about narcotics in the schools according to the reporter, Carter B. Horsley. The chairman of the school board admitted that, although there have been "very frequent problems at the school," which has about 1,800 students, the entire district has only two security guards. They are used to keep heroin pushers out of the school area.

Ironically, a meeting was to have been held the next night to discuss how children in the neighborhood might be protected from drug pushers.

A neighbor, describing the dead youth as an "exceedingly respectful boy . . . ," concluded, "I don't understand," a comment that reflects the questioning that goes on in all adults' minds when confronted with the end result of experimentation with death-dealing drugs.

In New York City by the early months of 1970, heroin use in schools had approached such proportions that press reports in *The New York Times* described the situation as an epidemic. "Heroin 'Epidemic' Hits Schools" was the headline for a front-page story by Thomas A. Johnson that continued for six columns on another page. He quoted a mother: "I wish she didn't have to go back to school," referring to her 15-year-old daughter, adding: "That's where she started using drugs in school." The woman was described as a garment center worker living in Harlem who had "watched her daughter closely at home but had not thought she had to watch her in school" too. She was terrified that her daughter might leave the rehabilitation center where she was receiving treatment.

The article provides another index of increased heroin use in schools, namely, the increase in the number of youthful pushers of narcotics.

On the basis of interviews with adolescent addicts, pushers, police, educators, and rehabilitation officials, the reporter noted that heroin is being sold in almost every high school in the city as well as in junior high schools, private and parochial schools, and is on the increase. The pushers are school-age dropouts, truants, and students, some as young as 11, and many of whom work at "cutting" the heroin at "factories" and packaging it in glassine envelopes. Some have even set up their own businesses. "As a result the death rate from heroin among teenagers has increased from 38 in 1964, to 79 in 1967, to 224 out of a total of 900 such deaths last year [1969]."

School officials find their "legal efforts to stop student pushers" a "revolving-door system," since the student addict pusher is arrested, taken to court, released on probation, and returns to school in a few days as "a folk hero, more popular than ever because he has 'beat the system'."

The commercialization of our culture provides a model and stimulus for the youthful addict to become a pusher as a way of paying for his habit. Since making money brings status as well, it is not surprising that "school and rehabilitation officials say it is almost impossible to convince a youthful pusher who has $200 in his pocket and is wearing an $80 pair of alligator shoes and a $50 cashmere sweater that selling narcotics is wrong . . . ," said John Fabio, a teacher at Charles Evans Hughes High School in New York. He recalled attempts to advise suspected school pushers, but they only say: "I'm making five times as much as you [teachers] do. Why should I quit?"

Evidence is provided to show some increase in heroin use by white youths in the city's treatment facility in Jamaica where youths from white families predominate. Also, the Federation of Jewish Philanthropies took steps to counter narcotics by calling for an interfaith program. The Federation stated that the number of Jewish addicts between 12 and 21 had greatly increased since 1965.

The reporter noted, however, that "most adolescent heroin addicts are still in the black and Puerto Rican areas"; and there is official recognition of the growing problem of narcotics in the schools. Pressures from fellow students and friends are cited as a primary reason for experimentation. " 'Shooting up' is considered . . . 'the in thing' and most insist that they can master the drug and will not become addicted. The first dose is often given free." Another factor that explains the increased experimentation is the availability—in varying degrees of potency—of $3, $2, and $1 bags, whereas previously the price per bag was $5.

If the ghetto addict-pushers had other opportunities for making extra money, for better clothes, they might not be so easily tempted to start on the heroin route. Nor would the temptation occur to such an extent if it were not so widespread in the ghettos. Material things that they have long lacked seem like worthwhile goals. They persist despite constant fear of being hurt or even killed by *their* pusher. A 15-year-old girl was robbed by policemen; run off the streets by older prostitutes when she tried to earn money their way; and finally got hold of some heroin but had to find some white powder to mix it with. "The only thing I could find was a roach-killer powder. I packaged it and went out dealing on the streets like always—in the streets and in a couple of schools." When asked what would happen to anyone "shooting" that stuff, she answered: "I only know what would have happened to me if I hadn't come up with some bread for the pusher and for my own stuff."

Such total lack of concern is an inevitable by-product of the enslavement that heroin addiction entails: enslavement to the drug and the pusher from whom the drug is obtained, plus the hounding by police whose arrest efforts have long been directed more against the addict-pusher than the nonaddict distributor or importer of large amounts of heroin. Also involved is a kind of desperation that seems to be a mixture of fear and a desire to be free of dependence on the drug.

A 13-year-old black addict begged the Director of the Addicts' Rehabilitation Center, James Allen, to bring him into the residential program. "If I stay in the day-care program I'll only go back on the stuff when I go home at night. . . . I've got to get away from it. I'm only fooling myself when I say I can stop using it." If awareness of what constitutes heroin addiction were more widespread, addiction would not be considered a crime. It would be recognized as a serious and contagious disease.

Allen summed up the ghetto problem: "We are dealing with the third generation of drug addicts in Harlem, while whites are dealing with the first," adding, "But you will see in months to come most of the money for narcotics prevention spent in white areas; experiments, like methadone, will be pushed in black areas." There are many reservations about methadone, because it is addictive, and we do not know what it does to the addict.

Failure to obtain funds has also hampered efforts at other schools; for example, efforts of teachers at Julia Richman High School to "establish a narcotic education counseling and referral program in cooperation with the Addicts' Rehabilitation Center in Harlem. . . .

Instead, the teachers, school guards and policemen go about taking drugs from students and arresting pushers entering the buildings. . . . We don't get the pill head or LSD kid here, . . . we get the heroin addict. They walk the halls, interrupt the classes, sleep with heads on the desks—some have lost consciousness." A Narcotics Education Action Committee has suggested the "formation of a therapy school that would remove addicts from contact with nonaddict students and give the addicted students supportive counseling and psychiatric help 'toward realistic goals and work involvement'," as well as a high-school education. There are still too few facilities for the treatment of school-age addicts, or, for that matter, for adult ghetto addicts.

John Fabio, the teacher at Charles Evans Hughes referred to earlier, summed up the feeling when he said: "Now that heroin is getting out of the ghettos, everybody is beginning to see it as a problem."[4]

## Why Drugs?

What drove Walter Vandermeer and other young heroin addicts and addict-pushers from the ghettos to drugs is fairly easy to understand if one has a firsthand knowledge of the conditions in the urban slums that predispose the young to heroin. It is painful to accept, since white America, which has a responsibility to change those conditions, has shown little evidence of a willingness to do so. For readers lacking firsthand knowledge of slum living conditions, the description by Mrs. Coretta Scott King provides an illuminating picture of the impact of ghetto environment on children. Speaking as a mother of four children for other mothers who are confronted with a sense of helplessness at being unable to provide security for their children, she notes that the poor "suffer not merely in material objects; they suffer want of confidence, of hope, and want of spirit." To this she adds:

> The black child, no less than others, needs freedom from fear. Yet, no matter how tenderly sheltered at home, in the streets the black child is exposed to crime and violence as a daily and not occasional scourge. White folks have recently expressed a rising concern about the crime that threatens them, and their fears are understandable . . .

Using comparisons published by the National Commission on Causes and Prevention of Violence, she notes that "the risks of physical assault are one in 2,000 for the white middle class; for upper middle-class suburbanites they are one in 10,000, but for the ghetto dweller they are one in 77! Yet physical assault is but a single aspect of the ubiquitous crime that envelopes the black child," adding:

Narcotics, prostitution, the numbers game, robbery, burglary, must
be added to the witches' brew. Aggravating even this deeply tragic
situation is the high visibility of crime in the ghetto. It is not sur-
reptitious and most of all it is practiced not only by elements tradi-
tionally identified as antisocial. In the ghetto the police engage in
forms of bribery and extortion so blatantly that small children are
accustomed to their making their illegal collection rounds among
shopkeepers . . . Crime enjoys a protected sanctuary in the ghetto.
It is very deliberately organized there as a big business because law
enforcement activity to inhibit it is minimal.[5]

There are some indications that blacks and Puerto Ricans are taking matters in their own hands to rout pushers from their communities. The Black Panthers have for some time had among their rules
for membership activity: "No Drugs." They have also engaged in
efforts to warn pushers identified by their nicknames that they are
wanted for "Murder!" The availability of heroin continues even as addicted GI's are returning to a country unprepared either to provide
treatment and rehabilitation or jobs when rehabilitated.

According to Ralph Blumenfeld, "Harlem, in despair over the
ravages of heroin, is reportedly ready to try again to intimidate and
drive out the pushers from bottom to top" ("Harlem Wars on Pushers," *New York Post,* July 6, 1971). Earlier there had been con-
frontations and "sit-ins" to protest lack of facilities for treatment and
rehabilitation. In the summer of 1968 there was a confrontation at
Harlem Hospital Center by the Council of Community Voices on
Narcotics, a coalition of organizations formed to fight addiction in
the black communities. Their complaint was that Harlem and other
black communities were receiving only "a trickle of the $29-million
granted by the Legislature for the state and city narcotics program
this year." Dr. Beny R. Primm, then the director of narcotics control
at Harlem Hospital and spokesman for the council, said "there is only
one rehabilitation center in central Harlem, adding: "And that is
fantastic since this is the largest area of narcotics addiction in the
world," according to *The New York Times,* July 25, 1968.

*The New York Times* of September 26, 1969, reported that "An
acute shortage of medical facilities confronts the addict in New York
City who wants to kick his habit and needs help." The shortage described in the article was in emergency facilities, detoxification facilities, and in treatment programs, either therapeutic or methadone
programs.

In the summer of 1970, the *New York Post* of August 14, 1970,
reported that administrators at Harlem Hospital were continuing to
search for more medical assistance in response to threats by a group
of 300 "drug fighters under the sponsorship of the United Harlem

Drug Fighters (UHDF)" who had occupied two floors of the hospital and were threatening to "kidnap" the doctors they needed. Also in 1970 the *Daily News* of January 14 reported a "sit-in" at St. Luke's to press demands for facilities to care for drug addicts under 18. The sit-ins were members of a group calling themselves Mothers Against Drugs. Their complaint was that "the city had failed to provide any service for teenage drug victims."

The shake-up of the New York City police force by Commissioner Patrick Murphy in late 1971 and the subsequent Knapp Commission hearings are an indication that white America is taking cognizance of the law-enforcement corruption that supports the availability of heroin in the ghettos. But this is only a beginning. And, as the authors of *Drugs and Youth* indicate, ". . . the combination of ghetto, heroin, and hopelessness is a particularly lethal one. As for our suburban youth, they may be angry, bored, resentful, disaffected, 'alienated,' frustrated, and so on, yet our society gives them much more attention than it gives to children of the ghetto; and therefore their chances of surviving heroin addiction are, on the whole, that much greater."[6]

What drove the middle-class youths described earlier in the chapter to a variety of drugs that caused their deaths is puzzling, especially if we confine the search for explanations to biographical data. If the deaths from drugs used by those adolescents were isolated instances, it might be accurate to say that they were unhappy, disturbed, or angry adolescents. But there are too many such deaths and too many different kinds of youths are involved to attribute them to their individual characteristics, personalities, and/or their families. Even if the latter factors were causally related to a greater or lesser degree, the fact cannot be overlooked that for decades drugs have been "pushed" in all of our advertising media as the solution to an extremely broad spectrum of problems of daily life. Nor can we dismiss the influence of the pharmaceutical industry, described as "The Legal Pushers" in a remarkable television program (August 30, 1970, part of NBC's Drug Alert Series), because of overproduction far beyond the medical needs of such dangerous drugs as the amphetamines, the barbiturates, and tranquilizers. Also implicated are physicians who overprescribe the above drugs. Additional details regarding the role of the medical profession and the pharmaceutical firms are included in Chapter V.

I recognize that adolescence is a period of turmoil and anxiety in a search for identity, and that this has been intensified in the post-World War II period as a result of the threat of nuclear annihilation, the cold war followed by two hot wars (one of which—Vietnam—is related to today's drug problems), and the erosion of our ethics and values. Nevertheless, if it were not for our society's acceptance of drugs and their ready availability, the youths who have already died might not have resorted to drugs.

That is not to imply that many of today's youths who are using drugs regularly, and whose studies or work—or both—are affected, may not have interpersonal and adolescent-adult relationship problems or other problems. However, even if those are relevant factors, they are not the *only* contributing factors. It is a dangerous myth to view what is frequently described as the "demand" for drugs as creating the availability, when in fact it is the availability that creates the demand, just as Madison Avenue has for a long time created demands for products we do not need. Vance Packard's *The Hidden Persuaders,* a best seller in 1957, provides voluminous documentation.

A word about the ease with which drugs are obtainable is important. In seminars, panel discussions involving high-school and college students, and adults, the students explain somewhat impatiently over and over again to the adults: "But the drugs are not that hard to get!"

Also implicated in today's widespread and increasing use of drugs is adult approval of drug use through acceptance of the continuing advertising in the mass media of drugs that are harmful or have not been adequately researched. Obviously, today's drug use by adolescents for nonmedical purposes has many meanings. Availability gives drugs an aura of acceptability. If I seem to be overemphasizing the role that availability plays, as well as the mass media advertising, it is because this is all too frequently overlooked. It is especially apparent in the use of the two drugs that are recognized to be the most dangerous, according to our present knowledge—alcohol and cigarettes. The length of time it has taken to obtain scientifically defensible data regarding the effects of smoking sufficient to make an impression on the tobacco industry and to reduce the amount and character of the advertising, as well as to reduce the smoking, provides confirmation—if confirmation is necessary.

In that connection, it should be noted here—although it is discussed in a later chapter—that we are not likely to have definitive results regarding marijuana for at least a generation, although some significant findings are currently available. (See Chapter VI.)

It is clear that a major drug problem today is that of heroin addiction. Although it remains a predominantly ghetto problem in the three urban centers having concentrations of blacks and Puerto Ricans, New York City, Chicago, and Los Angeles, there are signs that it is spreading throughout the country. How this picture will change when more GI's return from Vietnam addicted to a far stronger heroin than is available currently in the United States, and do not get into the limited treatment programs available, is of concern to many Americans and should be of even more concern to our Administration in Washington. Reports of returning GI's and their difficulties in getting jobs and, if addicted, with treatment, suggest there is likely to be an increase in drug-related problems.

Although it is generally recognized that the use of drugs for non-medical purposes is a symptom of what is wrong with American society and of increasing lack of confidence in our government to solve our major problems once the recognition is affirmed, emphasis in present control efforts is still focused on the symptom—not the roots.

It is time, it seems to me, to reexamine critically the effectiveness of the method of control that has for so long guided the country's efforts to solve the problems of narcotic addiction. The cost of heroin makes criminals out of persons who should be considered as patients in need of a special kind of treatment—a form of treatment that has been found to be successful in western countries most closely resembling ours, notably England. In three successive reports, in 1955, in 1963, and in 1965, the New York Academy of Medicine has described and recommended an approach that provides the only hope of solution. Details of that plan have been available in New York City since 1955, with the publication of the first of three reports on *Drug Addiction* by the New York Academy of Medicine's Committee on Public Health, followed by two additional reports, *Drug Addiction II* and *Drug Addiction III,* published in 1963 and 1965 respectively. Additional details within a comparable frame of reference are found in a remarkable as well as authoritative and comprehensive social-psychological study of young heroin addicts in New York City. I refer to the book: *The Road to H: Narcotics, Delinquency and Social Policy,* by Isidor Chein and his associates, published in 1964. Notwithstanding the ready availability of this material based on critical examination of the history of narcotics control and a social study of young heroin addicts together with an objective presentation of a social policy designed to make possible effective and humane solutions to heroin addiction, seemingly a veil of secrecy has prevented their study, discussion, and application while the present punitive, law-enforcement method of control continues wastefully and ineffectually. Treatment facilities—even methadone maintenance treatment programs—are woefully inadequate, in particular in neighborhoods where the majority of addicts are to be found. And their long-range effectiveness has not yet been proved.

What is even more shocking is the failure of present methods of control to prevent the spread of the contagion of heroin in the only way this can be prevented, by taking the profits out of the production and sale of heroin. Both the Academy of Medicine's Committee on Public Health and the social scientists who participated in the Chein

study agree that addicts vary, hence treatment needs to be individ-
ualized. A brief summary of the Academy's concept of treatment
follows:

> Any program of action for control of narcotics addiction, the Acad-
> emy has maintained consistently, should embody a rationale and a
> policy. In the Academy's view, addiction is an illness, an illness that
> spreads and may become a mass disease or epidemic. In this spread,
> the addict is a potential transmitter: in this instance, not of an in-
> fectious agent, but of a narcotic drug. Addiction is therefore both a
> medical and a public-health problem. An economic element, vast
> profit in illicit traffic, underlies perpetuation and spread of drug
> addiction . . . To the extent that addicts are under medical super-
> vision, the flow of narcotics will be diminished, and the black market
> volume will be reduced, with impact on the illicit traffic. Thus it
> follows that the policy should be to bring the addict under medical
> supervision for treatment and to prevent the spread of addiction.[7]

Also relevant is the Academy's statement that "all efforts to deal
with the spread of drug addiction have had the character of "nibbles"
at the problem. "What is immediately necessary," the Academy believes, "is to apply a procedure that will bring all addicts under medical supervision." This method of control has long been advocated by
Alfred R. Lindesmith, noted sociologist and authority on drugs, whose
book, *The Addict and the Law,* available in a paperback edition,
should be read by youths and adults alike. His book and *The Road
to H: Narcotics, Delinquency, and Social Policy* by Isidor Chein et al
are invaluable in providing understanding of the roots of today's drug
problems. Especially relevant is the following excerpt from Chein's
book.

"We are not suggesting that any addict automatically be given all
the narcotics he wants and, in effect, abandoned to his addiction. We
are not even suggesting that every addict be continued indefinitely on
at least maintenance doses. We are saying that:

> every addict is entitled to assessment as an individual and to be
> offered the best available treatment in light of his condition, his
> situation, and his needs. No legislator, no judge, no district attorney,
> no director of a narcotics bureau, no police inspector, and no nar-
> cotics agent is qualified to make such an assessment. . . .

> Addicts have been known to lead productive and useful lives as
> long as they were free of harassment.

The authors add:

> Drug use breeds on certain forms of human misery. The major
> problem posed by narcotic addiction is not at all the problem of get-

ting people to stay away from narcotic drugs. It is the problem of getting at the sources of such misery. Unless and until we have got to work with a will to do something effective about coping with them, we will not have begun to touch on the real problem of narcotics addiction.[8]

While the New York Academy, Lindesmith, Chein and his associates differ in some of the details of the plan all too briefly outlined above, all agree on the necessity of having the addict under medical and public health treatment. Additional details of this approach are included in later chapters, especially Chapter VIII.

The plan briefly outlined above, to view heroin addiction as a sociomedical problem under public health supervision has applicability to the marijuana problem. The persistent advocacy of legalization of marijuana on the part of adults who base this on allegations that it breeds disrespect for the law do not understand how our laws operate under the present administration and particularly with respect to dissent guaranteed by the Bill of Rights. Nor do they understand the basis for the very real disrespect many of today's youth have for adults based on the failure to solve major social problems, or even to show signs of wanting to do so, on the part of a majority of adults. Illustrative is the fundamental one of ending hunger and its evils once and for all: high infant and maternal mortality rates, other dangers of prematurity, brain damage or the underdevelopment of the brain due to pre- and postnatal malnutrition.

It is my belief, based on a number of research studies involving participation by adolescents that it would be possible to plan a nationwide, longitudinal study of the chronic effects of marijuana use on adolescents and preteens physiologically, psychologically, and sociologically and obtain meaningful participation of adolescents. In order to obtain a sufficiently large and representative sample with a control group, it would be necessary to have penalties for possession of marijuana for personal use only removed. Involvement in the research would require of the participants and initial health examination together with a depth interview for the purpose of obtaining social history data. Thereafter these would be arranged periodically. In recognition of the participants' contribution to the research, laboratory examination of their marijuana supplies would be available without charge as would any of the related services that might flow from the health examinations and/or the sociological interviews.

It should be noted that confidentiality along with freedom from punishment for the possession of marijuana for personal use would be guaranteed. It is anticipated that the launching of such a research project would do much to convince adolescents that adults are genuinely interested in their health and welfare. In a nationwide study,

mobility would not mean that a participant had to drop out of the
study. Additional aspects are presented in Chapter VIII. More specific details are premature until widespread acceptance of the idea has
been gained. I should make clear that dropping penalties is not the
same as legalization. The major objective of the proposed research
plan would be to ascertain the effects of long-range or chronic use of
marijuana so as to be in a position to make a wise decision. Adolescents, I find, respect this kind of approach to a controversial problem
in which sufficient and scientific fact as to harmlessness or harmfulness of a drug is adequately researched.

One more objective is important. In reporting regularly for examination and interview, and having their drug samples examined adolescents would be protecting their own health and, in addition, contributing information to the common pool of drug knowledge. The
importance of the laboratory examination hardly needs stressing,
particularly in view of recent findings from examination of illegal
"street drugs that showed that "STP (2.5-dimethoxy-4-methylam-
phetamine), a very dangerous drug that even experienced users reject is being sold as mescaline." Mescaline, a milder form of LSD, has
been used instead of LSD since the "chromosone-damage scare."[9] I
have known adolescents who use mescaline with marijuana. The researchers involved in this discovery express concern that "new and
inexperienced users may be taking STP, and believing it to be mescaline . . ." Nor is this the only hazard due to contaminants in
street supplies of drugs. *Science.* Feb. 27, 1970. p 1276.

Another development that points up the urgency for research as
to the effects of marijuana significant, is a report by Dr. Charles
Winick, an authority on drugs and Director of the American Social
Health's Association's Program in Drug Dependence and Abuse,
New York, to the effect that there has been a steady extension of
drug abuse to younger and younger age groups, adding:

> Now there is shocked awareness that it has reached the very young
> indeed. In the last few years abuse of a variety of chemical sub-
> stances, from glue to heroin, has been growing among children of
> the middle years—those between ages eight and twelve and, in
> school terms, between the third grade and junior high school.

Winick attributes this receptivity to "mood-modifying chemicals" to
parental encouragement of early dating, some parents even encouraging going steady at nine or ten. "Millions have purchased sexy man-
nequin dolls for their daughters." Play with these dolls "centers on
changing her costume in preparation for a date [also 'turned out
appropriately']. Fantasies about dating and sex may take the place of
daydreaming about future motherhood, which used to characterize

the years of doll play . . ."[9] Other contributing factors are the rock records with their sexual message expressed explicitly, fierce competition for school grades, and the easy availability of pills in the family medicine chest.

Under the circumstances, it would seem even more important to initiate the proposed marijuana study. A byproduct of such a study might stimulate a comprehensive and critical examination of other hazardous drugs used and abused by adults as well as children and adolescents, e.g. the amphetamines, barbiturates and tranquilizers that are widely advertised and freely prescribed by the medical profession, according to the authors of *Mystification and Drug Misuse* (1971) discussed in Chapter V: *The "Legal Pushers."*

CHAPTER II

# *What Are the Alternatives?*

If youthful ghetto addicts, with little expectation that there will be improvement in their life situation in the near future, are pleading for help to rid themselves of heroin addiction, which provides an escape from despair and pain, there must be times when middle-class drug users have momentary flashes of questioning whether they too should not consider getting off drugs. Since we are creatures of habit—and habits are easier to form than to break—it is important to stay with the questioning long enough to ask yourself: Why am I using drugs? and What are drugs doing *for* me? The questioning will return time and again. If I am right that there is that kind of questioning from time to time, but you let it pass quickly because it is easier to continue doing the "in thing" than to change, I would like to suggest an experiment. Try to arrest the momentary flashes of doubt and ask yourself, frankly and honestly, just why you are using drugs and what you get out of the habit.

I realize there are many motives for using drugs. Whatever yours may be, ask yourself whether in using drugs you are getting what you expected. At times, when you are perhaps getting a little jaded with the experience, try another experiment: Try to recall the circumstances under which you first became curious about drugs, curious enough to experiment, and just how it happened that you began to use drugs. If you work hard enough at the second experiment, you should be able to answer the following questions: Did you come to a firm decision on your own that you were going to take drugs? Were you influenced by peers who were taking them? Did you let the situation, so to speak, make the decision for you?

For instance, did you go to a party at which you knew drugs would be available and you thought it would be fun *just to experiment?* Or were you feeling pressure to use drugs because you were uncomfortable being different? In answering the questions, it is not going to be easy to be honest. The pressure, if any, will come only from yourself. The brain is the most amazing and remarkable aspect of a human being and is capable of doing things—without benefit of any drugs—

that seem almost miraculous. It is also one of the most neglected. Scientists are only just beginning to gain some understanding of its capacities, and insight into the dimensions of human potential. William James, one of the most eminent of American philosophers and psychologists, "once estimated that the healthy human being is functioning at less than 10 percent of his capacity." Margaret Mead quotes a 6 percent figure, whereas the estimate of Dr. Herbert A. Otto, the author of the article cited below, is 5 percent or less. However, more than fifty years passed before William James's idea gained acceptance and then by only a small proportion of behavioral scientists. More recently, additional facts about human potential have come to light:

> There is evidence that every person has creative abilities that can be developed. A considerable number of studies indicate that much in our educational system—including conformity pressures exerted by teachers, emphasis on memory development, and rote learning, plus the overcrowding of classrooms—militates against the development of creative capacities.[10]

Dr. Otto cites an eminent Soviet scholar and writer, Ivan Yefremov, in *Soviet Life Today,* 1964:

> Man, under average conditions of work and life, uses only a small part of his thinking equipment . . . If we were able to force our brain to work at only half of its capacity, we could, without any difficulty whatever, learn forty languages, memorize the large Soviet Encyclopedia from cover to cover, and complete the required courses of dozens of colleges.

Does this suggest that someday man will be able to take over the work of the computer? Dr. Otto comments that the statement by the Soviet scientist is hardly an exaggeration. It is the generally accepted theoretical view of man's mental potentialities. Work is now under way to tap that "gigantic potential." There is even evidence that owing to the pollution of our environment, our sense of smell, ability to see color, and other senses have atrophied to the point that we perceive "less clearly, and as a result we feel less—we use our dulled senses to close ourselves off from both our physical and interpersonal environments."

Can drugs really be more exciting than trying to expand one's own consciousness (the cerebral cortex), since it is man's consciousness that separates him from other mammals? Everyone has experienced a surge of energy in an emergency. And most people know of retired persons who suddenly become creative in a variety of fields in which they had not even had training.

The kind of communing with yourself that I am suggesting provides an open door from which you can imagine yourself free not merely to reconsider, but to consider *anew,* what you would like to do with your life. It is imperative for your future and the future of the nation that today's youth, all youth from the cities, the rural areas, the ghettos, and the affluent suburbs, begin to create doors that open out to a process of learning how to become individuals again.

It is particularly essential for your generation because of the exposure to television, the full impact of which has not been adequately studied; and because, since the 1950's, the idea that there is a "youth culture" separate from the adults has become widespread. Those who talk about a separate "youth culture" and believe in its separateness from adult culture may not be aware of the extent to which your generation has been sought after and influenced by Madison Avenue. In fact, no past generation has been so pursued by the mass media to buy products, lured by creating fads that become the "rage" so that more products may be sold. For the moment, I am omitting the very different and more constructive role of the mass media—in particular, television—in informing you of the hypocrisy, the evil, and the apathy of adult society with respect to solving the major problems of the nation.

By the early 1950's, Madison Avenue had developed a program based on research to capture the teenage market for profits. One man, the late Eugene Gilbert in particular, a sort of genius in marketing, and head of his own company, the Gilbert Marketing Group, wrote in *Harper's* (November 1959): "For some fifteen years, I have been carrying on an intensive study of the adolescent in the role where he is most distinctly himself—as a consumer." In that article, "Why Today's Teenagers Seem So Different," he presented his views on the basis of a poll of 6,000,000 teenagers by 5,000 teenage pollsters whom he employed on college campuses and elsewhere. To adults "dissatisfied with the younger generation," Gilbert suggested that "instead of bemoaning the queer ways of their young, it might be more useful to take a hard look at the society in which they are growing up. After all, we made it for them." With slight modifications, the suggestion has applicability to today's experimentation and use of drugs, since it is adult society that is implicated.

In the pages that follow, evidence is included to show that, far from rebelling against the Establishment in using drugs, you are following the cues provided by that Establishment. In short, you are doing "their thing," with little awareness that it is *their* thing, and not yours.

Just how intensive the pursuit of teenagers by Madison Avenue has been was illustrated in a 1962 *New York Times* article: "Whether it's a food ad, a clothing ad, even a headache remedy ad, chances are it will be awash with teenagers. The teenager is very much on Madison Avenue's mind." The reporter noted that the advertising industry's sudden "fascination with the teenage market is a result of cold calculation and careful research," research involving study of population charts and a comparison of the rate of growth in numbers of teenagers with that of the total population. Of special relevance is the statement that "Besides constituting the fastest-growing segment of the market, teenagers also form the segment that is most easily reached by advertising and is most susceptible to its blandishments."[11] In a subsequent chapter, another aspect of the influence of today's mass media with respect to drug use is presented.

Today's youth may not be aware of the relationship between advertising and stepped-up profits for the pharmaceutical industry, with the result that drugs were being prescribed by physicians on the strength of subtle and persistent pressure with all of the techniques of modern advertising at their command—drugs inadequately researched and being recommended for a variety of problems of daily living.

The authors of *Mystification and Drug Misuse* make clear that to promote both types of drugs, the prescription and nonprescription drugs, the pharmaceutical industry has engaged in "mystification," which they define as "the communication of false and misleading explanations of events and experiences in place of accurate ones, explanations which serve one party at another party's expense . . ."[12]

Few drug users today are aware of the degree to which the Establishment is implicated in your use and abuse of drugs, through increased availability and acceptance in the mass media. Or to put it in simpler terms, the society you think you are rejecting is the very society whose models you are taking for your own. In the early 1960's up to about 1965, when marijuana was just becoming a kind of fad among the so-called "elite" on college campuses and then was copied by high-school students who in talks with me identified the groups as "artsy-craftsy" students, it was just that and remained thus until about the latter part of 1968.

In the intervening years, young persons who had been engaged in civil-rights struggles in the South and later in comparable struggles in the North were seemingly unable, without more direction from adults, to continue this kind of activity. Further, dissent on college campuses and a rising tide of antiwar activity in that period were greatly diluted for most youth by a new interest, almost a fascination, with the new "hippie" activities and life-styles that were conveniently promoted by the mass media with all of the remarkable techniques at their disposal.

In essence, it was a new version of the earlier promotion by the mass media of the sex revolution, the social origins of which are described in detail in this author's book, *The Teenager and VD: A Social Symptom of Our Times.* The failure to grasp the motivation behind the mass media's campaign of distraction is owing largely to lack of understanding of our history, and the degree to which the mass media are controlled by and act as an arm of the Establishment.

The same type of distraction followed the awakening of the American conscience and the remarkable muckraking that occurred during the first decade of the twentieth century, brilliantly described in Vernon Parrington's last volume of *Main Currents in American Thought,* Volume III, but particularly the last chapter: "A Chapter in American Liberalism," pp. 401ff., in which he describes the awakening of the intellectuals to the deception that had blinded them as to the course that American society was taking: "The journalistic muckrakers had demonstrated that America was not in fact the equalitarian democracy it professed to be, and the scholars supplemented their work by tracing to its historical source the weakness of the democratic principle in governmental practice."[13] It was this reawakening of the American conscience and the popular support, thanks to McClure's ten-cent magazines, that stimulated intellectuals to look further. *An Economic Interpretation of the Constitution of the United States,* by Charles A. Beard, is the most significant product of the intellectuals of the period and makes clear that the Constitution was not intended to promote democracy; rather it was intended to provide the basis for a form of government that would protect those with property from the factions that would be likely to result from "the various and unequal distribution of property."[14] This was considered by the Founding Fathers to be a result of "the diversity in the faculties of men . . ."[15] (Additional details will be found in Chapter III.) The introduction of psychology during World War I—Freudian psychology—also described in this author's book mentioned earlier—served the same purpose then as the campaign of the mass media in the current period: to focus on private not public needs.

It is pertinent to raise a question:

In light of both the commercialization that must stimulate drug use among youth, and this on the part of our most prestigious profession, where should efforts of the public—in particular, parents, educators, and adults involved with adolescents—be directed?

Both adults and youth should examine critically this commercialization of our society, which for so long has encouraged materialistic values, and drugs as solutions to problems, in the name of helping our economy. (The 1950's saw a serious recession at a time when it had been predicted that the boom would continue indefinitely.)

In rejecting the middle-class materialism of parents and adults generally, some teenagers have substituted new and "hip" forms of materialism stimulated by the same commercial forces. Misunderstanding and stereotyping on the part of adults and adolescents occur through the failure to see that both forms of materialism have a common core: the conspicuous display of possessions for status in the suburbs is not essentially different from teenage rock music that sells millions of records; the use of drugs, the clothing fads, travel, and the drugs and ever changing life-styles—all of which make profits for others than youth, including those derived from both the "legal" and the "illegal" drugs.

More than ten years ago, I began a talk by debunking two twentieth-century myths that have gained not only widespread popularity but have even been dignified by pseudoscientific support. "One is that man's nature is essentially evil and the best that society can do is to keep this in check. On the contrary, available evidence from biology, psychology, and sociology makes clear that man's nature is potentially good and that since his behavior is learned it can also be changed. It has become both profitable and fashionable to emphasize man's capacity for evil. One has only to examine current art, literature, the drama, and the mass media to confirm this observation."[16] In the intervening decade, this myth has become even more deeply embedded in American culture. Youth, in particular, have been affected by this.

"The other myth is that of neutrality. It is especially prevalent among social scientists, and crops up in many adult-adolescent dialogues about drugs as 'Don't moralize, give us the facts.' I refer to an assumption that there is a kind of 'no-man's-land' designated as a neutral zone, from which social scientists can examine our problems objectively, that is, without expressing a point of view. This neutrality assumes that there are always two equally valid or beneficial sides to every question, or that one can study or examine behavior without a point of view; or, to make it absolutely clear, without indicating on which side you stand. The late Robert S. Lynd, in a remarkable book (first published in 1939), stated: 'A good scientist has a point of view. He holds it subject to constant correction, but without a point of view he is no scientist, and as a teacher he becomes simply a walking equivalent of an encyclopedia or a colorless textbook.' "[17]

I *have* a point of view about drug use and since it has been offered only indirectly up to this part of the chapter, I will make it explicit here, so there will be no doubt about it. I am most concerned about today's extensive use of a wide variety of drugs, many of which have an actual, others a potential, danger, especially for the young. My view as to whether a drug is harmful or harmless is the following. It is taken from an article published by Henry Brill, M.D., who was then (October 1968) Vice-Chairman, New York State Narcotic Commission:

> Generations of experience have shown that there is no such thing as a drug which is both free of risk and still pharmacologically active. In this sense all drugs must be considered guilty until proved innocent. The type and the extent of risk must always be determined first. The hazards of a drug must be fully evaluated and its safety established before it is released for general use.[18]

I am concerned in particular about the waste of human potential in those youths who remain on drugs for a considerable period of time. One thing is clear: It is not necessary to take drugs to show one's difference from or outright rejection of, or contempt for, what is usually referred to as the Establishment, or the power elite who control our country. It is still possible to reject the materialistic, anti-human values of current-day American society and live and work by the values professed by Americans, but which are conspicuous by their lack of application. Millions of adolescents and adults are doing just that—and more. They are showing their difference and their rejection through positive actions, actions too numerous to cite here, but which are included in the chapters dealing with solutions.

In turning to drugs—whether to expand consciousness, to search for identity, or to rebel against the hypocrisy of that segment of the adult world that refuses to see the evils of racism, and hence blocks efforts to end the evils; that refused to press for an end to the war in Vietnam and to outlaw war as a solution to international problems; that refused to end, once and for all, hunger and the poverty that fosters it, demoralizing innocent children and their parents—you are doing precisely what the Establishment would like youth to do: to retreat into private worlds of your own and not offer any resistance to either our present national or international policies. In addition to evidence already presented, I would like to add as confirmation one more striking piece of evidence: It is not hard to find a correlation between an increased availability of drugs and dissent on college campuses against war-related research, continuation of the war and its extension in Indochina. There is also evidence that heroin is now flowing into the United States from Indochina, where—if we wanted to—we could stop it tomorrow, since it could go on only with our knowledge and assistance.

I am well aware that I am not likely to convince you at this point. However, it is my hope that by the time you have finished reading the book, those of you who use drugs regularly will at least feel that it *is* worth your while to consider alternatives, and those of you who are experimenting will take into consideration what your peers have learned: that it is easier to get on drugs than to get off. For those burning with curiosity to begin experimenting, I can only repeat what every adolescent has told me who was able to get off drugs:

"Don't start!"

CHAPTER III

# Today's Drug Abuse Could Have Been Prevented

No social problem of any magnitude emerges "out of the blue." There are signs, rumblings, and clues that trouble is brewing long before a serious problem comes to the surface. Unfortunately, the persistence of a policy of indifference to the welfare and rights of a majority of the American people, in contrast to the tender, loving care bestowed upon the welfare and rights of property, that is, of those who control the economic resources of our country, prevents serious consideration of the early signs of problems. In the last two decades evidence has been accumulating that points to a callous neglect of the need to improve the condition of our cities, in particular the slums that had already begun to deteriorate before World War II. With the flight of the middle class, urban decay was intensified. More significant in terms of the failure to examine the post-World War II rumblings is the oblivion that developed with respect to the needs of the poor, in particular the poor from our minority groups, and specifically the failure to take note of the postwar heroin addiction of high-school students in the ghettos of New York City.

It is not surprising, therefore, that few middle-class Americans were aware that:

In the first few months of 1951, no less than 260 boys and girls, their ages ranging from fourteen to twenty, were admitted to Bellevue Hospital in New York City because of addiction to heroin. Other children were killed by the drug and never made it to the hospital. They were all from Harlem and they made no headlines in the New York papers, let alone in Boston or Seattle.[19]

In fact, one of the authors of the above had found it necessary earlier to reiterate what should have been well known:

Again and again it must be stressed that drug addiction in America overwhelmingly plagues the poor Negro and Puerto Rican.[20]

36

Even fewer were aware that heroin addiction was then widespread among high-school students, chiefly in the city's vocational high schools; or that an extended study of narcotics for the State Legislature had been completed in 1952 by former Attorney General Nathaniel Goldstein, who concluded:

> The health, welfare and safety of our citizens is threatened by a spreading menace. It must be eradicated by all means at our command. The problem of narcotic addiction is of ancient vintage. It strikes at us in recurring stages. Now it has reached our young, in growing numbers. Once and for all, we must rid ourselves of the scourge.

The Legislature did little except to pass a law requiring that instruction be provided in the state's public schools. Unfortunately even this was not implemented. A *New York Times* editorial (May 14, 1970) from which the above references to the study were taken, concluded that, "as a result, yesterday's wind has become today's whirlwind. A state that was worried two decades ago about rising teenage arrests connected with narcotics—the concern in the Goldstein study —must now worry about rising teenage deaths connected with drugs."

It is hard to understand and even harder to explain why nothing came of the Goldstein study, the law passed by the State Legislature regarding drug education; why nothing came of the various hearings, commissions, and even a U.S. Senate Committee in the 1950's. The only logical inference that can be drawn is middle-class indifference and lack of concern regarding drug use so long as it affected only ghetto youth.

One need only compare the hysteria that occurred when it became apparent that marijuana had invaded the suburbs with the lack of attention to the long-standing abuse of heroin as well as marijuana and other drugs in New York City ghettos. Only when in the 1970's there was rising concern that heroin was being used by middle-class youths was there beginning concern with heroin addiction in the ghettos.

The myth that prevented awareness of heroin addiction as a problem when it involved only ghetto children and adolescents is still all too prevalent, namely that the major drug problems are those affecting middle-class youth. That includes still another myth, namely, that today's drug abusers are primarily youths, obscuring evidence that a much larger proportion of adults are drug abusers, in particular of the amphetamines, barbiturates, and tranquilizers, even if drug use and abuse of alcohol and tobacco are omitted.

In the same period, Isidor Chein, Professor of Psychology at New York University, and his co-researchers began what still is the most comprehensive and authoritative social-psychological study of narcotic addiction in New York City.

> It happened that, toward the end of the first year of our investigation,
> a major hearing was to focus on the narcotics problem in New York
> City. It was already widely known that we have been collecting data
> on drug use in the juvenile population of the city. A few days before
> the hearing, we began to receive visits from representatives of certain
> public and private agencies. Each of our visitors had the same re-
> quest, . . . in essence: 'I have to testify at the hearing, and I will
> surely be asked how many addicts there are in the city. I hope you
> can tell me.' We explained the nature of our statistics; they referred
> to individuals involved with narcotics—most of them known to have
> taken narcotics, and the bulk of the remained could be safely as-
> sumed to have done likewise. . . We pointed out that we were deal-
> ing with only three of the five boroughs; that our figures referred to
> *known* cases; and that, to arrive at the true figures, one would have
> to multiply our statistics by an unknown factor—perhaps two, or
> three and one-half, or seven. We were both amused and dismayed by
> newspaper reports (subsequently verified in the published record)
> of the testimony given by each of our visitors. . . . And—this is the
> crux of the matter—apparently no one thought of asking them how
> they arrived at the figures.

> The question of what to do about drug use is highly controversial.
> Certain issues of fact are germane to this controversy. In the past
> few years, there have been many hearings by various bodies—a com-
> mittee of the United States Senate, special legislative commissions
> in various states, and local government agencies. At these hearings
> there are always many witnesses to testify on the facts.[21]

Nothing came of the numerous hearings by local and state government agencies, special commissions in various states; even from a
committee hearing of the U.S. Senate. The authors conclude that the
experience referred to above provided them with some perspective as
to the quality of the facts presented at the various hearings and commissions. In that respect, history is repeating itself; we still do not
have the true facts about drug misuse. And the mass media have contributed little in this respect.

Nor is it likely that we will have the facts we need as to the extent of
the experimentation, use, and abuse of drugs, unless and until the use
of drugs for nonmedical purposes is recognized for what it is: a sociomedical and public-health problem rather than a criminal problem to
be solved through law enforcement efforts. That in no way implies
that law enforcement should not continue its efforts in controlling the
illegal traffic, in particular finding the distributors at the top. A *Wall
Street Journal* editorial, "New Priorities on Drugs" (July 7, 1971),
noted:

One of the self-defeating features of U.S. efforts at control of drug abuse has been an emphasis on police methods aimed at controlling the supply and use of dangerous drugs. There need hardly be any greater evidence submitted to show the failure of this approach than merely to cite the dimensions of the drug problem that has developed in this country. Drugs have become the leading cause of death for people between the ages of 15 and 35 in New York City, for example.

A question in my mind is whether the persistence of an approach that has not only criminalized the drug users, but has increased their number and led to the spread of drug abuse in communities small and large throughout the country, as described in Chapter I, may not be owing to the fact that heroin use continues to be largely a problem in the urban ghetto. The term, *drug abuse* is fully discussed and defined in the section preceding list of references.

Another question that needs to be raised is whether the seriousness of the heroin addiction problems in New York ghettos in the 1950's would have failed to be recognized had they involved teenagers from middle- and upper-class families. Apparently, it did not occur to middle-class America, some members of which must surely have been aware of the increased availability of drugs in the urban slums, that there was a possibility the contagion of drug use might spread to the suburbs, so isolated had affluent America become from problems of the urban poor, a majority of whom are black and Puerto Rican. It should be noted that it was not until 1962 that Michael Harrington's *The Other America: Poverty in the United States* was published.

A brief summary of the origins of heroin addiction on the part of high-school students and other youths in the 1950's dispels a prevailing myth that drug abuse and addiction are primarily individual and personal problems. It is no accident that narcotics should have become available in New York City ghettos in the post-World War II climate that denigrated the ideals and goals for which the war had been fought. During the war hopes were raised among those Americans who had never been granted equality of opportunity, that improvement in their lives would be forthcoming, particularly in the economic sphere, since, so long as the war lasted, there was full employment, necessary to win the war.

Nor is it accidental that signs of problems occurred in that period. The war, coming on the heels of the Depression of the 1930's, left many unsolved problems, in particular those affecting the poor in our large cities, blacks and Puerto Ricans, for example. The promise of implementation of our democratic ideals that were prominent during the fighting came to naught once the war ended. No sooner had President Franklin D. Roosevelt's death occurred than a new and different war was declared—a cold war—an ideological war—in which the

enemy was communism—a new and different form of government
seen as a threat rather than a challenge to our form of government
that would enable the peoples in the two great powers to decide for
themselves. The cold war was followed by McCarthyism, the Korean
war, and Vietnam. Those wars, in particular the cold and the hot wars,
particularly Vietnam, from which we have not as yet recovered, have
brought our country to a state from which we cannot recover except
by ending the war and beginning to solve the three problems with
which American people are concerned today: the war in Vietnam,
the state of our economy, and heroin addiction.

In a recent Gallup Poll (released June 1971) drug addiction was
cited as the number three national problem of concern, after Vietnam
and our economic problems, on the basis of a survey of those over 18
in more than 300 communities. It is significant that racism, which is
integrally related to all three of the above problems—or "race relations," as it appears in the poll—was rated as the fourth problem.
What is particularly relevant for this book is that "while the percentage of persons citing the war and the economy as the most important
national problems remained about the same as in a previous survey
in March, the percentage of those naming drug addiction as the top
national problem doubled since March. . . ."[22] Reasons given for the
increased concern over drugs were press and government reports, in
particular those reporting use of heroin by American servicemen in
Vietnam.

Thanks to the democratic climate during the war and in the postwar period before the 1950's, many reports, commissions, and cri-
tiques of the shortcomings of our democracy were published. They
pointed to the possibility that implementation of our democratic
ideals would be a result of the war. That it did not materialize despite
the raised hopes of our minority groups is the result of a climate that
began in the early 1950's in which the right to dissent was seriously
challenged, as evidenced in the inquisition brought about by Sen.
Joseph R. McCarthy.

## Roots of Drug Abuse in the Ghettos

Among the reports mentioned above was that of the President's Commission on Higher Education: *Higher Education for American Democracy* (New York: Harper & Brothers, 1947), which documented
that it was in low-income families and in low-income regions "least
able to provide them [children] with a good education at home or in
school *that the greater number of children are being born today."* The
report documented the fact that American society has failed even "to
provide a reasonable equality of educational opportunity for its

youth," and that "the kind and amount of education . . ." depended "not on their abilities, but on the family or community into which they happened to be born or, worse still, on the color of their skin or the religion of their parents." A comparable situation was found with respect to health in a study, "Child Health Services and Pediatric Education," the first nationwide survey covering child health services, which reported that "children in isolated counties receive one-third less medical care than those in or near cities. . . . States with low income and few services have a larger percentage of their population than do high-income states."[23]

In that same period, an article in *The New York Times Magazine* by John J. Corson made it unmistakably clear that "despite two years of high national income since the end of the war, government—federal, state and local—is burdened with a vast relief problem. . . ." In human costs, the 11,000,000 persons receiving some form of government assistance included 1,775,000 children under 18, and represented "millions of aged, orphaned, blind, sick, and unemployed who even in good times were not earning enough to meet the cost of rent, food, utilities, and clothing."[24] (See also Appendix A.)

Three years later, A. Delafield Smith, writing on the subject, pointed out that "the inalienable right to life, liberty, and the pursuit of happiness were rights that human beings used to have at the hands of nature . . . rights they would continue to enjoy if not deprived of them." It has therefore

. . . become necessary for our society to take appropriate steps to assure the existence of these natural rights, to implement them in the positive sense, to underwrite the economic life of the individual members of society, and to preserve their liberties in the process.[25]

There was already then a serious increase in school dropout rates and unemployment of our youth, in particular among blacks and Puerto Ricans. Indications of those problems were available long before the confirming studies were initiated and made public.

Over and above the problems just described that should have alerted our leaders to not one but many youth problems, was the increasing failure of our economy to provide employment for adults as well as for youth. In a report of the joint committee on the economic report of the 81st Congress, it was made clear that "the size, need, and economic circumstances of the low-income families have not been adequately appraised in recent years." The report noted that "in an economic system geared to mass production there must be mass consumption if severe economic dislocations are to be avoided." The low-income families were described as having lived "at levels below even the most conservative estimate of the minimum for health and decency."[26]

It is apparent that in every aspect of their lives the children in those families, estimated at that time to be 10,000,000, or one fourth of the nation's families, were severely deprived. It is, therefore, not surprising that the nation's urban areas, and especially the ghettos, should have been plagued by high rates of school dropouts and unemployment. Although noticeable in the 1950's, action, chiefly in the form of conferences, committees, and reports, did not take place until the 1960's when President John F. Kennedy stated in November 1960, as he announced the formation of a special committee on youth employment: "I am particularly disturbed over the plight of the nearly one million out-of-school and out-of-work youth." Several months earlier, at a conference on Unemployed Out-of-School Youth in Urban Areas, sponsored by the National Committee on Children and Youth, James B. Conant, president emeritus of Harvard University, had warned that the situation represented "social dynamite." Secretary of Labor Arthur Goldberg had called it "the most dangerous social condition in America," and Secretary of Health, Education, and Welfare Abraham Ribicoff, "a terrible waste of our youth." (See also Appendix A.)

Youth unemployment was recognized as an extremely serious problem and one that might well be the last straw; for some young people, it might even "mark the turning point toward delinquency."

That this was to continue to be a serious problem was also recognized in view of the jump in the birth rate after World War II when 26,000,000 new young workers were entering the labor force.

"It was recognized that while Negroes make up only one-tenth of our labor force, they account for almost one-fifth of all unemployed, denied access to apprenticeship, on-the-job and other training programs. . . ."[27]

Earlier, Conant had stressed that "a youth who has dropped out of school and never has had a full-time job is not likely to become a constructive citizen of his community. Quite the contrary, as a frustrated individual he is likely to be antisocial and rebellious. He may end as a juvenile delinquent."[28] (See also Appendix A.)

Those are the youths in our urban ghettos who are likely to seek, through drugs, forgetfulness or compensation for the emptiness and lacks in their lives. According to Isidor Chein and others, many heroin addicts in their study were delinquents before they became addicted to heroin. (*The Road to H.*)

In preparation for the conference on unemployed out-of-school youth, "a few special studies were conducted in slum areas of large cities to find out what the facts really were. . . ."

In a slum section composed almost entirely of Negroes in one of our largest cities, the following situation was found. A total of 59 percent of the male youth between the ages of 16 and 21 were out of school and unemployed. They were roaming the streets. Of the boys who graduated from high school, 48 percent were unemployed in contrast to 63 percent of the boys who had dropped out of school. In short, two-thirds of the male dropouts did not have jobs. In such a situation, a pupil may well ask why bother to stay in school when graduation for half of the boys opens onto a dead-end street?[29]

Conant cites a special study in another city that revealed an even worse state of affairs. In a slum area of 125,000 inhabitants, mostly Negro, "a sampling of the youth population showed that roughly 70 percent of the boys and girls were out of school and unemployed."

The reader who is well informed about *today's* unemployment of youth may wonder why so much emphasis is placed on past unemployment. It is to emphasize the long-term neglect of conditions in our urban slums that persist and are not only "social dynamite" but perpetuate the racism that is at the core of the present urban blight and is the soil in which drug abuse and addiction flourish. My purpose is to call attention to conditions in the urban ghettos that favor the ready availability of drugs. Because of the lack of employment for ghetto youths, despite the fact that the 1950 drug problems were ignored by the Establishment and the middle class, drug addiction and abuse began and continue to be predominantly ghetto problems. The factors described by Mrs. Coretta Scott King in Chapter I make clear why.

Conant's conclusion with respect to unemployment is equally applicable to solutions to our current ghetto drug problems. "To improve the work of the slum schools requires an improvement in the lives of the families who inhabit these slums, but without drastic change in the employment prospects for urban Negro youth, relatively little can be accomplished."[30] Unfortunately, although some improvement has taken place in education since the early 1960's, the employment situation has not improved. On the contrary, as the war in Indochina continues, employment possibilities for all youth are decreasing. As our economic problems grow more serious, they are beginning to affect even middle-class youth.

Many readers may have forgotten and many youths will not have known a best seller published in 1957, *The Hidden Persuaders,* which was a critique of the "huckster methods" by which Americans were influenced by psychological and psychoanalytic techniques—to buy things they did not need, among other things. Many who read the book may not have been aware of the relation between the beginning of motivational research for commercial purposes and weaknesses in our economy, which can be summed up briefly as a chronic, long-term, and progressive inability to provide employment for all our people, young and old, who are willing and able to work. The problem was and continues to be especially acute for our youth, as has already been made clear.

In his book Vance Packard noted a problem that is of even greater concern today:

> A good many of the people-manipulating activities of persuaders raise profoundly disturbing questions about the kind of society they are seeking to build for us. Their ability to contact millions of us simultaneously through newspapers, TV, etc., has given them the power, as one persuader put it, to do good or evil "on a scale never before possible in a very short time."[31]

However, Packard himself did not grasp the full import of his investigation until a year later when he wrote an article: "Resurvey of 'Hidden Persuaders,'" subheaded "A critic of huckster methods shifts his concern to consumers." It is time, he says, "to reexamine our materialistic set of values."

In that postscript to his book, Packard refers to an economic recession that had inspired "a great many Americans to begin reexamining materialistic values by which our society has increasingly been living. . . . Today (1958) I see their [the hidden persuaders'] efforts as symptoms of the strain our system is undergoing. Our system itself, which has been impelling us more and more to conform to a materialistic set of values, needs examining, I now see, along with the symptoms." He states that "our leaders, from the President down, are admonishing us to 'buy' more. What we buy is not as important, seemingly, as the mere fact that we buy. A New York newspaper recently headlined the fact that a 'rise in thrift' was 'disturbing' the Administration."

Packard emphasizes: "All this straining to keep the sales charts rising is responsible, too, for proposals in marketing circles that Americans should be constantly encouraged to modify their moral reservations toward a hedonistic (or 'live it up') attitude toward life." He notes that marketers were being admonished to reassure consumers that "the hedonistic approach to life is the moral one and that frugality and personal austerity are outdated hangovers of Puritanism."[32]

To the serious lacks for children in low-income and minority groups, already described, must be added the lacks and strains that lead middle-income children to alienation and drug abuse, or dependence, the term used by the World Health Organization. (Dependence is used as synonymous with addiction and has the advantage that it makes no distinction between physical and psychological dependence.

See section following Chapter IX for elaboration of the definitions of terms relating to drug abuse.) The 1962 Annual Conference of the Child Study Association, which was based on the theme, "Youth in Search of Significance," is a good illustration of beginning signs of unrest, dissatisfaction, and alienation of youth in all groups and classes that already had begun to be noticed. Unemployment, although affecting chiefly black youth, was not without its effect on middle-income youth. In addition, increasing automation was beginning to make work less and less significant.

In the general session of the Child Study Association Conference, "The World They Live In: The Social and Cultural Climate," Dr. Charles Frankel, Professor of Philosophy, Columbia University, described youth's troubles today in search for significance as "just part of our troubles in building a society in which there are rational, human, and significant activities to pursue." As a guide to solution, he recommended "a somewhat greater interest in social reform, a somewhat more systematic interest in social reconstruction; and most of all, a much greater willingness on the part of all of us to engage in political controversy." (John Gardner's organization, Common Cause, is a step in implementation of this kind of recommendation.) Making clear that there is no special way to deal with problems of youth, Frankel concluded: "If there is crime, there will be juvenile delinquency. If there is adult passivity, there will be youthful passivity. If there is adult irresponsibility, youth will go us one better. In the end, we can, I think, repair our condition of youth only by repairing our own condition."

In a session on "The Illusions and Ideals of Belonging" at the Conference, Graenum Berger, consultant, Community Centers, Federation of Jewish Philanthropies, New York City, commented on "the fragmentation and rootlessness of our society, describing youth in the early 1960's as "escaping from an incomprehensible world

. . . which does not seem to be able to resolve the problems of hunger, overpopulation, race relations, war, and possibly world destruction. And like his contemporary adult, for whom youth has always partly modeled himself, he has turned to the pill and the machine rather than the human being for comfort and salvation . . . We seem to be pulling away rather than helping our teenagers toward more permanent rootings in contemporary life.[33]

To the above should be added concepts of child rearing, in particular on the part of the middle class, that emphasized permissiveness rather than responsibility as a result of uncritical acceptance of Freudian psychology, which stressed happiness almost to the exclusion of responsibility, out of a genuine fear that any frustration of children would lead to neurosis. That fear is largely responsible for permissiveness in standards of sexual behavior that has been abetted enormously by the mass media, a permissiveness on the part of adult society that is by no means unrelated to drug abuse, as the article by Charles Winick in *The PTA Magazine,* referred to briefly at the end of Chapter I, makes clear.

During that period psychoanalytic theory was overemphasized in child rearing; Allen Wheelis, socially oriented psychoanalyst, makes the point in his book, *The Quest for Identity,* that popularity as a goal has been substituted for achievement. In a culture in which we are seduced to gratify our every wish as if it were an urgent need, many adults are unable or unwilling to institute controls in their own lives and, hence, fail to do so for their children.[34] Why that is so is complex. Wheelis explains it in Chapters III, "Character Change and Cultural Change," and IV, "The Emergent Social Character."

It begins to look as if the fragmentation of our society today, its depersonalization, and the erosion in the quality of our lives—in particular the quality of the nonmaterial aspects that we have only begun to identify—are causally related to today's drug use. That means that if the factors described above—all too briefly, considering their importance—had been taken into consideration, we would have become aware and hence could have prevented the widespread use of drugs for nonmedical purposes. That would have required taking note of the use of drugs by adults.

## Rhetoric in Place of Action

The studies described in this chapter have pointed up the unfinished business of our democracy. Unfortunately, there were few results from those studies. In the more recent period, we have the same situation: Our government has appointed commissions to study the causes of race riots, crime, and the drug problem.

Their findings have resulted in indictments of our society that also point to solutions. They seem to be forgotten once the reports are made public. Of the reports, the most outstanding in terms of the social roots of today's drug abuse problems is the Kerner Report, which Tom Wicker describes in his introduction as ". . . an extraordinary document . . . What had to be said has been said at last . . ."[35] Especially relevant to this book is documentation of the conditions in our slums—which have become predominantly black—that make widespread heroin addiction understandable and that contribute to the alienation of a proportion of middle-class adolescents out of a sense of frustration at the gap between understanding the evils that are literally spoiling the quality of human life and the incredible failure of our government to do anything about eradicating the evils except for occasional rhetoric. As Mrs. Coretta Scott King has so eloquently put it: "No one step-at-a-time process can suffice . . . A total program which would simultaneously strike at all the deficiencies is the only effective solution. Had the nation begun a gradual process a hundred years ago it might today have simple remnants to deal with."[36]

Racism, solutions to which involve peace and an end to poverty, goes to the roots of what is wrong with American society, affecting the white majority as it does all our minority groups. It goes to the roots of today's drug abuse problems. There is a clear relationship between the apathy and indifference of adult society vis-à-vis solutions to racism and the use of drugs on the part of the young. Adults did not provide needed support for the continuation of youth's enthusiastic participation in the "Mississipi Summer," a participation that involved courage, idealism, conviction, and hardships, as well as exposure to brutality, jail, and in some cases beatings and death. Partly out of a lack of awareness of the meaning of rapid social changes, which the young felt more keenly than adults, partly because of an overestimation of youth's understanding of the world and their capacity for sustained and responsible action in this arena; and partly through lack of concern and inaction, adults have lost an opportunity to provide models and guides for youth in what might have been a tremendous force in stimulating social reform, as was suggested by the reports cited earlier in the chapter from a conference on the topic, "Youth in Search of Significance."

In that connection, Wheelis notes that the young have become weary and skeptical. They are seeking something that "will provide what values and goals have always provided . . . they want something that will last." But, says Wheelis, "What can substitute for values except other values? What can function as goals except other goals? . . . There is, indeed, no escape from values and goals . . . The effort to diminish the stress occasioned by accelerating change cannot eliminate goals and values. It can, however, force them to become subjective."

It is precisely in adopting subjective values and goals that the young become vulnerable to the seduction of drugs. In not understanding the crisis of values and goals on the part of youth, the soil was prepared for the influence that the availability of drugs has had on adolescents.

Wheelis makes clear that in becoming subjective, "one abandons the tasks of the world and bends one's efforts upon one's self. One gives up hope of changing the world and resigns one's self to the alteration only of one's reactions," adding:

This is the current guise of defeat. One seeks adjustment, a flexible personality, warm interpersonal relationships; and most particularly one cultivates an increasingly sensitive awareness of one's inner life and conflicts. But the energies of man drive for discharge; the direction of flow is outward. The cultivation of only one's self can command but a small fraction of one's potential motivation. The larger part remains dammed up, a reservoir of restless discontent.[37]

In seeking solutions to drug abuse it is essential to keep in mind that these are stirring times in which one person such as Ralph Nader has been able to effect a pathway to social reform and change that has endless possibilities for meaningful activity.

The recent publication of *America, Inc.—Who Owns and Operates the United States?* provides a panorama of possibilities that should stir the imaginations of youth and adults alike. The author's description of "establishment" should endear the book to youth. In Chapter I, "A Tour Through a State of Concentration," they conclude: "The examples are almost endless of how public government gives favored treatment to giant business. Public government and private government have joined together in tight embrace. This is the 'establishment'."

They conclude their book: "Concentrated power lies at the core of much of the unrest, injustice, and unresponsive government that beset us. Until it is removed we can fiddle with this and that, but true progress will elude us."[38]

If we really believe that today's drug abuse is a symptom of a society in crisis, then unless we are willing to tackle the roots of the problem, let us stop talking of solutions that are not worthy of the name. (See also Appendix A.)

CHAPTER IV

# Marijuana: Symbol of a "Turned-On" Society

In September 1966 Robert Coles, well-known child psychiatrist and author, in a review of two books on drugs, raised questions about the logic of the classification of marijuana as a narcotic while the psychedelic drugs, particularly the most powerful one, LSD, were enjoying "comparative freedom." (Fortunately, marijuana is no longer so classified by the federal government, but states have yet to change their laws regarding this, and LSD is now classified as a "dangerous drug," and has the same illegal status as marijuana.) His questioning also was based on the seriousness of heroin addiction in comparison with marijuana, noting that not many powerful people in Congress were concerned about narcotics but were more likely to be interested in "the faddish drug 'trips' and the antics of a very small minority of our college youth."

> There is a ready market in this country for sly and foreboding news about college youth. Particularly of late many students have demonstrated their idealism and their curious resistance to the blandishments of a society that is—certainly for them—in the chips. Those students, too, may be a minority; but a well-known one they are. For certain people it is a perfect set-up; why not discredit one minority with another, make civil rights workers or peace demonstrators drug-high or worse?

In reviewing one of the books, *One in Seven: Drugs on Campus* by Richard Goldstein, Coles states that the "figures one in seven—who mainly try marijuana—is an admitted conjecture . . ." and "can be discredited on a number of counts, making clear that it does not really matter how accurate his percentage is." The "gist of the author's message," he wrote, "is that more students are giving marijuana a casual try, with most of those who do quickly calling it quits, and only a few proceeding to stronger drugs." Coles, an extremely sensitive observer and interpreter of youth, sums up his estimate of marijuana use by college students thus: "I rather suspect, though, that we are in for no great and convulsive upset (or inspiring upturn, either) from our youthful fanciers."[39]

In the *Saturday Review,* two discerning sociologists began an article by writing:

> The use of marijuana has leaped from the peripheral zones of the society to its very center. Just a few years ago marijuana was limited to the ghetto scene, jazz circles, and the highly alienated young in flight from families, schools, and conventional communities . . . Our children, in being casual about drugs—particularly casual in their acceptance of them and their promises—far from being in revolt against an older generation, may in fact be acknowledging how influential a model that generation was.

A second factor, they indicate, is that "marijuana as an idea and possibility has become a widely available cultural fact; this article in itself, is a part of this." In confirmation, the authors, themselves young adults, make the point that for their generation and older generations, exposure to marijuana "even as a concept was highly limited. To gain a knowledge of marijuana beyond a few jokes about jazz musicians, one had to journey to the margins of conventional society, and to experience the drug one had to carry hard-earned credentials. Now, seemingly all at once, it has become a proper topic for the mass media. Major magazines discuss the problem at length, TV comedians and filmmakers have at it."[40]

From the above citations and other evidence I have come to the realization that marijuana was not in widespread use by middle-class youth until probably sometime in the latter part of 1967 or early 1968. This is confirmed, in part, by a survey of high-school students undertaken in November 1966 in my own community of Great Neck, N.Y. The survey was conducted by school officials and the *Guide Post,* the student newspaper of one of the community's two high schools. It was stimulated in part by the arrest of a few teenagers for using and selling marijuana and by national police estimates "that anywhere from 15 to 50 percent of the teenagers in any suburban community may be experimenting with marijuana." The survey included questions on the use of barbiturates, amphetamines, hallucinogens such as LSD, DMT, and marijuana, cough syrups containing codeine, and glue-sniffing. Questions were answered anonymously, and the survey was based on answers by 2,587 students out of a total enrollment of 2,800.

Pertinent to this book is the finding that "8 percent of the student body in grades 10, 11, and 12 had used marijuana" and that of these "only 4 percent were sufficiently interested to say they would definitely try again." Marijuana had the largest number of experimenters, and "other hallucinogens, in spite of Timothy Leary's *Playboy* statements, were rejected by over 98 percent of Great Neck's teenagers." A summary of the survey was reported in *The New York Times* of February 17, 1967.

A question was raised as to the low proportion of students using the hallucinogens: "Why, one might ask, is the percentage so low in spite of *much publicity otherwise?*" [Italics added.] It was noted that "more than 54 percent of those who have never experimented said they did not want to endanger their health; 28 percent said they are too busy and interested in other things, while 9 percent were deterred by concern for their parents, and 9 percent did not want to be arrested. This might further deny a *Look* implication that the main deterrent to the misuse of drugs and narcotics was 'legal'." A total of 9.35 percent admitted using drugs.

Except that it was, so far as could be ascertained at the time, the first such survey, the special relevance for this book is the added evidence that during the beginning of 1967 publicity about marijuana use became widespread. This coincides with the beginning of an ongoing interest in the drug problem on my part, when I was invited to serve on an Advisory Committee of Nassau County, which, in 1967, became the Nassau County Drug Abuse and Addiction Commission, the policy-making body for a far-flung program of treatment and rehabilitation services. I have been a member of the Commission since then.

The character of stories on drugs and their influence in stimulating experimentation and use of marijuana are the subject of this chapter. An illustration of that publicity is an extensive article in *Life* magazine (July 7, 1967) entitled: "Marijuana: Millions of Turned-on Users," with twelve photographs of users smoking the drug in various situations. The article covered eight pages and included significant information. Unfortunately, the value of the information was greatly minimized by the seductive manner and tone of the article, which began:

> Almost overnight the U.S. was embarked on the greatest mass flouting of the law since Prohibition. Marijuana, a mild euphoric drug known and used throughout much of the world for centuries and long a part of the bohemian scene in the U.S., suddenly has become commonplace on college campuses, among intellectuals and suburbanites, and—most worrisome of all—even among subteenagers. Some authorities estimate as many as 10 million Americans have tried marijuana at least once, and the number of users is increasing rapidly.

The estimate of 10,000,000 could not be verified then or since; nor are we likely to unless we cease to view it as a matter for law enforcement.

The *Life* article continues with evidence to confirm the statement that "the number of users is increasing rapidly."

> Just how fast can be gauged from the fact that New York police last year seized 1,690 pounds of "pot"—17 times as much as in 1960—and concede this is only a fraction of the total coming into the city.

It is hard to understand how the amount seized can be used to confirm an increase when from my vantage point, based on my knowledge of the problem, it is more logical and, I am convinced, more accurate, to infer that the seizure and the increase in the marijuana coming into New York City presumably represents increased availability of the drug to stimulate its use by youth. This is supported by Coles's observations already noted, and by those of the authors of the *Saturday Review* article.

Some of the information in the *Life* article is helpful in providing a better understanding of how the contagion of marijuana smoking is spread. "The use of marijuana is encouraged by rock 'n' groups, by the editorializing of underground newspapers and by 'psychedelic shops'." Mixed in with information that is valid is a kind of emphasis likely to stimulate interest in drug use on the part of a young adolescent who is lonely, or has some school problem, or is just bored. Stating accurately that the effect of the drug varies with the smoker and his mood, also the potency of the marijuana and the setting, a scene, presumably a typical one, is described as follows:

> In a circle of smokers there can be hilarity, a rush of talk or a solemn, ritualistic silence; almost never is there violence or trouble. Most smokers think of marijuana as a kind of lens through which they see more clearly, more beautifully. But this feeling of a heightened awareness of something that heads find hard to share with anyone but with other heads, and from this comes their reverence for each other, their ironic detachment from the "straight" world, their zeal to turn every one on.[41]

The term "heads" is usually reserved for those young people, hippies or college students who, as described by Kenneth Keniston, make drug use a central focus of their lives. In his article from which the above is taken, he provides additional details regarding differences between alienated youth and committed youth as to drug use.

In addition, comments such as the following in the *Life* article could be irresistibly alluring to the impressionable young mind:

Those who pursue getting high to the point of "dropping out" find that an elaborate subculture has been constructed for them to drop into. Once inside it, they invariably adopt the apocalyptic vision of the underground, which preaches death to "repression" and soon for the American culture as it stands. Thus the allure of marijuana goes far beyond the subtle effects of a smoke. There is great exhilaration in joining a band of missionary-outlaws who are convinced that their psychic revolution will bring about the betterment of man.

As if the foregoing exerpts were not sufficient to "turn on" many a teenager who is temporarily angry with his parents or teacher, or just in a restless mood, the article notes that there is "a whole chorus of cult-heroes. . . . the Beatles, Donovan, Bob Dylan, the Jefferson Airplane, Allen Ginsberg, the booming underground press—their message is all the same: now is the time to turn on."

The rest of this lengthy article contains information that is accurate and useful, including comments from six adults (a sociologist, a psychiatrist, a legislator, a biochemist, and two "crusaders," one pro and one anti) whose views about marijuana are quoted. Also cited are arguments for and against legalization. However, after the glamorous introduction, it is doubtful whether the susceptible or just plain curious adolescent, would not soon be on the telephone talking it over with a friend, or making plans to get marijuana.

The last page of the article includes a piece: "Stoned kids think they can handle it," which describes the hazards: Referring to a group of 14 youngsters "California-affluent junior-high-schoolers, good students and normal children whose parents thought they were off on a picnic," the article quotes them as boasting that they can handle marijuana use and will not go on to heroin. . . . , "this is childish bravado, heightened by the marijuana itself. The kids who are so sure they can handle it do not understand the nature of what they are dealing with, nor its effect on their attitudes and outlook."[42]

Lest it appear that the above article is atypical of the mass media approach to drugs, analyses of other articles follow that provide some idea of the role of the mass media in stimulating middle-class adolescents to turn on to marijuana and other mind-expanding drugs. While these articles reflect divergence of adult views and confusion regarding drugs, they should stimulate critical reexamination of the concept of what is considered newsworthy. Discussed below in this chapter are two articles of a 5-part series by *The New York Times,* based on a nationwide survey on January 8 to 12, 1968, inclusive. These articles raise the question: What is neutrality in reporting "news" about social problems? Is it—or should it be—essentially different from the concept of neutrality discussed in Chapter II.

Much that passes as "news" in the mass media, using the term in its most comprehensive sense to include rock lyrics, movies, etc., is far from neutral as the excerpt from "Children of the Drug Age," in *Saturday Review* of September 21, 1968 makes clear:

Referring to an increase in marijuana, the authors raise the question as to "who or what are the carriers of marijuana culture?" and conclude that the "infectious carrier turns out to be aspects of public culture that are fully legitimate and social relationships that involve persons very much like the potential marijuana user," adding that

> Much of the imagery of marijuana use is transmitted increasingly in the mass media, especially the mass media that serve youth. Lyrics of popular songs refer to the drug itself or the drug experience in barely coded terms often coded just enough to establish an illusion of membership among the listeners . . . Elements of the music are described as having an additional message *if* the hearer is properly turned on. More crucial is the fact that the media frequently in articles and programs designed "to inform" and "warn" an adult audience, as well as to excite its fantasies, provide an ideology and a definition of self that makes marijuana use legitimate; it is sometimes tied to "a new spirit," a "new honesty," a new quest for substantial values and experiences, a children's crusade organized around the reinvention of Rousseau, Thoreau, and Lawrence. In this way, the mass media provide not only a basis for legitimization of the use of pot, but also a structure of rationalizations for the fact of use.[43]

The opening paragraphs of *The New York Times* article, of January 11, 1968, the fourth in the nationwide survey referred to above, entitled: "The Drug Scene: Many Students Now Regard Marijuana as a Part of Growing Up," describes the prestigious college town of Amherst, Mass., now graced by head shops, where all the exotic paraphernalia of the marijuana cult is sold. There is also a casual description of Harvard Law School students gathering for an evening of conversation, music, and pot. Thus does the reporter provide a kind of social acceptance for marijuana use. In addition, it is noted that "drugs, particularly marijuana, have become for many students a part of growing up, perhaps as common as the hip flask of Prohibition." The reporter continues:

> While drug use has been expanding over the last few years, *students and high school and college officials agree that it has increased sharply since the intensive coverage given to drugs and the hippies last summer* [1967] *by the mass media.* [Italics added.]
> "There's no doubt this thing has increased since the summer. There were articles on the East Village in *Esquire, Look* and *Life* and this provides the image for the kids," said Donald W. Miles, the principal of Horace Greeley High School in the Westchester suburb of Chappaqua.

In addition to an increase in drug use, marijuana in particular, the use of drugs "cuts across all types of young people. In the past, younger students were introduced to drugs, 'turned on' by upperclassmen. Now, students on many campuses say, freshmen arrive already smoking marijuana or taking it for granted that it is part of the college experience." The reporter also notes that

Marijuana—grass in the current campus phrase—has spread from avant-garde, artsy-craftsy colleges, through the Ivy League and the schools in big cities, through universities with transplanted New Yorkers, to campuses all over the country. It also has spread to exclusive prep schools such as The Hun School in Princeton, N.J., and Phillips Academy in Andover, Mass., and on to high schools in places like Brattleboro, Vt. and Cedar Rapids, Iowa.

On the basis of interviews with students, the reporter indicated that,

. . . while many drug takers appeared to be troubled, many were not. Furthermore, many students who gave little evidence of being particularly thoughtful seemed to be sampling drugs simply because they were available, or because they were considered sophisticated or daring. Others were smoking marijuana because it was the social thing to do, like sipping a cocktail.

That was in contrast to the views of psychiatrists and school and college administrators who described students who use pot regularly as tending "to be rather bright and rather introspective, to often have personal or family problems, and to be alienated from both the values of the adult world and from those of his fellow students." The reporter commented "but it is this type of students that psychiatrists and administrators are most likely to come in contact with, resulting in what sociologists term a 'biased sample'."

Throughout much of the rest of the article, bizarre instances of middle-class youth using drugs are described in a fashion, more likely to stimulate interest in experimentation and finally to provide social acceptance than to inform. Such episodes are interspersed with the views of a medical student studying drug usage, who expresses concern about today's drug use:

The frightening thing about these kids is that they'll take anything anywhere. I used to think it wasn't so much different from what we did at that age, but this is really dangerous.

and the *Times* reporter comments:

Indeed, it is the teenybopper's ready acceptance of drugs such as methedrine [also a very dangerous drug], which can induce psychological dependence, compulsive, sometimes violent behavior and intense feelings of paranoia, which has hastened the break-up of the Haight-Ashbury hippie community in San Francisco.

Also in contrast to the somewhat exotic and daring descriptions of adolescent drug use are the views of Dr. H. R. Kormos, a psychiatrist in Westport, Connecticut, who provides a picture of the "pervasive depression," the "feeling of nothingness" on the part of middle- and upper-class youth in that community: "There is a very genuine feeling," according to Dr. Kormos, "that life has little to offer them, and they speak continually of the dreariness, the drabness of everyday life." He suggests that "particularly with marijuana, the mystique and ceremony of sharing the drug may impart a sense of belonging and identity that may be more important to the student than the effect of the drug."[44]

The expressions of depression and the "feeling of nothingness" of the Westport adolescents are not unique to that community. They reflect a widespread lack of belonging and identification with adult society on the part of affluent youth arising out of their having been prevented from becoming a significant part of the society. That feeling results, in large part, from a tendency in American society to underestimate the capacity of even young children to function in socially significant roles appropriate to their age and development.

The third article in the *Times* series: "A Growing Number of America's Elite are Quietly 'Turning On': Some Seek Insight; Others Sexuality," conveys an unmistakable and overt acceptance of drug use. Beginning with a long, drawn-out, and somewhat theatrical description of a Thanksgiving party to make the point that status adults were using marijuana socially, the reporter notes that "adult America is 'turning on' in ever-increasing numbers."

What the *Times* national survey found is that:

> While still a small minority of the population, more and more on-the-way-up and already successful adults were using marijuana and hallucinogenic drugs. Many more were found to be using barbiturates to relieve tension and amphetamines to capture a feeling of limitless energy.

The reporter's acceptance is heightened by the intriguing and alluring tone of the writing, and the selection of illustrations of adult drug use and abuse. He notes:

> In their search for something mystical, or for their lost feelings, or for a way out of their boredom, the adults have taken for their own much of the trappings of the hippie subculture.

It should be noted that what individuals say they gain from the use of hallucinogens is subjective. We do not have studies or the techniques by which to obtain objective verification of "new insights" gained from drug use that can be attributed to the drugs and drugs alone.

The reporter cites a trial lawyer who "got started on the amphetamine-barbiturate kick by taking sleeping pills when he could not sleep before an important trial; then, finding that he was not alert for his clients, he started his day with an amphetamine."

Dr. William McGlothin, psychologist from the University of California at Los Angeles, suggests a further incentive to use hallucinogens, such as LSD. He is quoted as stating that these drugs "may also stimulate a new-found interest in music, art and nature, a sort of aesthetic Head Start for artistically deprived adults."

Citing the frequent use of amphetamines and barbiturates by successful professional people to help them cope with the pressures of detailed living, the reporter adds:

Most of the adults interviewed were particularly articulate. They also held good jobs and appeared self-confident and assured. Despite their material success, however, they said they were alienated from the mainstream of American life. . . . Although they may have considered themselves as nonconformists, their nonconformity was not reflected in their daily lives. Few were involved in causes—civil rights or Vietnam—and few took part in community activities. . . . Many of the men held jobs they did not like, despite their success. One lawyer who regularly uses marijuana and LSD said that "after my first [LSD] trip it was unmistakably clear that this was not what my life was about—real estate law. Other people, probably stronger people, could come to this conclusion without drugs, but I couldn't. Suddenly I didn't feel that I was put upon this earth to reduce landlords' real estate taxes."

The reporter comments that the man "had given up the law and gone into book publishing."

Although that illustration may seem to be a compelling justification for drug use, it could also be argued that other avenues exist for solving some of the crucial problems of meaningful work. There are friends to speak to, professionals to consult. There is also no reason to believe that the insight he attributed to LSD might not have been obtained, or even deepened, through a human contact from which he might have added to his self-confidence. In any case, as I noted in connection with an observation made by the psychologist, Dr. McGlothin, how does one prove that the drug caused the insight?

Much of the rest of the article describes marijuana and LSD parties and "trips" with a strong emphasis on sex. The adult participants claim that drugs, including the amphetamines, "lend a spice to sexual relations that their own imaginations do not."

The reporter concludes:

> There is usually a scandal when the sons and daughters of the white-collar drug users are caught smoking pot or using LSD. But, the Times survey showed in many cases that parents and children shared the same values.

He also notes that "when the 'elite' are caught, the authorities sometimes wink at their transgressions."[45]

The above article would not have been included for analysis if not for the fact that adolescents still model their behavior on that of adults. If the media had been interested and concerned, evidence of drug use and abuse by adults could have been discovered earlier. There is evidence that much of the rejection of adult society on the part of some adolescents is, in part at least, owing to awareness of the "hypocrisy" they attribute to adults—and rightly so, for becoming hysterical and outraged at their use of marijuana when they (the adults) have for a long time been using drugs classified as "dangerous," as well as using and abusing alcohol and nicotine. It may well be that adult use of marijuana is of fairly recent origin except in bohemian circles. But abuse of prescription drugs such as the barbiturates, the amphetamines, and a wide variety of tranquilizers, and even dependence on some of these, are not new. In that connection, Erik Erikson is cited as follows: "Our younger generation makes overt what the older generation represses."

As in the case of changing sex mores in what I describe as a sex-drenched, violent, and increasingly pornographic society, which cannot be attributed to youth, today's drug use was learned from adults. In that respect, there is no generation gap—if in fact such a gap exists outside of the mass media, in particular in television, though there is a serious credibility gap.

An understanding of how youths' behavior is often a continuation or extension of adult behavior, though differing in its outward form, might do much to lessen the mutual hostility and self-righteousness of each as they view the other. It might also help each side to reexamine its basic values and premises about drugs as well as other problems.

It should be noted that the first two articles in the *Times* series regarding the drug scene were informative and useful for both adolescents and adults. The first one, "Americans Found Increasingly Oriented Toward Wide Variety of Drugs—Usage by Youth Grows the Most. Dependence Grows," also cites views of authorities as well as reporting on the status of drug use, that is, that not only the slums are involved and that the use of alcohol, barbiturates, and ampheta-mines by the middle class provides evidence of a subtle change away from the Protestant ethic and the pioneer spirit. That should not be surprising in view of the successful efforts on the part of advertising to win Americans over to the spurious values of wasteful consump-tion, living today without concern for the future, and an acceptance of hedonism—a fun psychology—as a way of life.

Alcohol is still the major offender and the drug abused by the largest proportion of the population. The use of tobacco is in second place with 80,000,000 smokers as against an estimated 10,000,000 users of barbiturates, amphetamines, and tranquilizers. As for the proportion using marijuana, the estimate based on the *Times* survey is 2,000,000 to 4,000,000 instead of the astronomical "millions" cited even by the National Institutes of Mental Health in its publica-tions. Dr. Richard Flacks of the University of Chicago stated that student activists rarely used anything more than marijuana, and that only casually.[46]

The January 9th article in the series is devoted to what is known scientifically regarding the misuse of drugs and a lag in research. The reporter also notes what has been a characteristic of the current drug scene from the very beginning, namely, the disagreement between experts. Additional study is urged to learn more of the effects of drugs. The article includes a chart listing the drugs, their medical use, if any, the symptoms produced, and their dependence potential.[47]

The last in the series deals with the illegal traffic and, except for a few instances of material as to how to smuggle in drugs, the article is, for the most part, a report of the law-enforcement activities of the authorities, as the heading and subheads indicate: "Nation's Illegal Traffic Is Valued at Up to $400-Million Annually." "New York Called Distribution Area." "Most Marijuana Smuggled from Mexico Lands Here, in Chicago or Los Angeles."[48]

The foregoing analysis of reports of drug use in the mass media is illustrative of the varied role that the media play: providing informa-tion as well as social acceptance along with, in some instances, a kind of fascination with drugs that seems to be designed to increase circu-lation, rather than to provide news.

The role of commercialism in contributing to an increase in drug use, noted in the *Times* article, quite aside from the enormous profits derived from the illegal traffic of drugs, attests to the strength of the basic value of our present society, namely, making money. I am referring to the "cashing in" on drug use in the "head" shops, the rock lyrics containing hidden and coded messages that drugs are "in" and are O.K.; the paperbacks that emphasize the influence of marijuana in enhancing sex, and, most important, the advertising of drugs to the general public. (Elsewhere, in Chapter V, advertising of drugs to the medical profession as well as to the public and its effects on a drug user are discussed.)

The article described below from a Long Island newspaper in the metropolitan New York area, *Newsday* (November 1, 1970), "Mary Jane Turns On the Profits," represents a concept of news, or information to the public that is at the same time helpful to parents as well as informative to youth. The article describes a firm that has become "big business" through distributing accessories to smoking marijuana, described in an earlier *Times* article (January 10, 1968). The article states:

> For those who think the $5,000,000-a-year pot industry is confined to Times Square or just the major cities, here are some of the places Cosmic Truth distributes its flavored paper, hash pipes and other marijuana-smoking gear: Pocatello, Idaho, Cedarhurst, Long Island, Skokie, Illinois, Mechanicsburg, Pennsylvania, Levittown, Long Island, Fairfield, Maine and Smithtown, Long Island. That's just a partial list of its outlets. If Cosmic Truth's rate of growth is any indication, dope accessories won't be just a $5,000,000-a-year industry for long. Cosmic started eight months ago with about 25 different head products. Today it has 75 and can't get new product catalogs published fast enough.

Reference is also made to "Headgear, Inc."—"The hash pipe people who have become so big in three years that they were considering going public."

# CHAPTER V

# The "Legal Pushers"

The drug culture finds its fullest flowering in the portrait of American society which can be pieced together out of hundreds of thousands of advertisements and commercials. It is advertising which mounts so graphically the message that pills turn rain to sunshine, gloom to joy, depression to euphoria, solve problems and dispel doubt.

> —SENATOR MOSS, chairman of the Senate Consumer subcommittee, requesting a study of the advertising industry. The *New York Post,* July 1970.

Tranquilizers have become a big business . . . a new national habit . . . The physicians have been sold. So has the country . . . Three quarters of a billion dollars are spent yearly by some sixty drug companies to reach, persuade, cajole, pamper, outwit, and sell one of America's smallest markets, the 180,000 physicians . . . The pharmaceutical industry alone can hardly be indicted for this inducement to increased drug usage. It is an American tradition that growth is good, and increased corporate earnings demand ever larger markets.

> —HENRY L. LENNARD, et al. *Mystification and Drug Misuse: Hazards in Using Psychoactive Drugs,* 1971

In spite of little justification medically, but with considerable harmful potential, the American pharmaceutical industry has "skillfully managed to convert" amphetamines "into multihundred-million-dollar profits in less than 40 years," James M. Graham reports in the January, 1972 issue of *TransAction.* "High profits, reaped from such vulnerable products, require extensive, sustained political efforts for their continued existence."

The Comprehensive Drug Abuse Prevention and Control Act of 1970 is a victory "over compelling contrary evidence on the issue of amphetamines," a victory that "could not have been secured without the firm support of the Nixon Administration. The end result is a national policy which declares an all-out war on drugs which are *not* a source of corporate income. Meanwhile, under the protection of the law, billions of amphetamines are overproduced without medical justification."

In opening the 1969 Senate hearings on control of drug abuse, Attorney General Mitchell "set the tone of administrative policy related to amphetamines" by agreeing they were "subject to increasing abuse" but that because of their *"widespread medical uses"* they are "appropriately classed under the administration guide lines . . ."

By contrast, the consensus among physicians currently is that "amphetamines are medically justified for the treatment of two very rare diseases, hyperkinesis and narcolepsy." However, only "a few thousand tablets" could cover the whole country's medical needs, a source of supply that could be made and distributed by the government "at very little cost," Dr. John D. Griffith of the Vanderbilt University School of Medicine testified. Dr. John Jennings, acting director of the Food and Drug Administration (FDA) also testified to the drug's "limited medical use," adding that it had "doubtful value" in controlling obesity.

Petitions filed by the American Public Health Association, the D.C. Public Health Association, and other organizations sought reclassification of the amphetamines to limit their production and distribution. This brought the reclassification of pep pills by the Justice Department into Schedule II of the 1970 Drug Abuse Prevention and Control Act earlier in 1971, thereby requiring the setting of production schedules.

*The Nation's Health* (the official newspaper of the American Public Health Association) in its December 1971 issue placed the APHA in the position that "by strengthening policing action over distribution, illegal diversion would be virtually eliminated." Accordingly, quotas should be set, based on "the anticipated needs of legitimate medicine, rather than on prescription policies of the past." These have not as yet been set.

Since some of the cost to the American people of the profits derived from the sale of dangerous drugs will not become fully apparent for a generation or more, it is urgent that we recognize the power advertising has gained in shaping our lives and that solutions be found to curb this power.

In the 1950's concern was expressed on the part of some physicians at the degree to which doctors were relying on the laboratory to make their diagnoses and on the pharmaceutical industry to provide the treatment. In this connection, Dr. Iago Galdston pointed out that in curative medicine, "it is the laboratory—not the physician—that makes the diagnosis, while it is the pharmaceutical house that provides the treatment." Dr. Galdston also noted that "the pharmaceutical and drug organizations are exhibiting a great deal of initiative in instigating, directing, and supporting research, naturally in the framework of their interests. They are also active in the education of the practicing physician."[49]

Almost two decades later, the role of the pharmaceutical industry is described as "redefining and relabeling as medical problems calling for drug intervention, a wide range of human behavior which, in the past, have been viewed as falling within the bounds of the normal trials and tribulations of human existence." Evidence of that is found in their ads in medical journals, in direct mail to doctors, and in advertising that goes directly to the general public. The practice has done much to stimulate the use of drugs by our youth. While the sale of all drugs has greatly increased, "the sale of psychoactive drugs has increased to a greater extent."

That practice, or mystification, as it is called by the authors of the above-quoted book, conceals the true role of the drug industry. The psychic or psychoactive drugs, according to the authors, have been used "for only a comparatively short time," and their action "tends to be less specific and more diffuse than that of other drugs in medical use. They not only alter body processes as do other drugs but also affect a whole complex of psychological and social processes connecting the individual with his physical and human environment." Whether the drugs are prescribed or self-administered, they tend to elicit "a broader range of unintended and unanticipated side effects, consequences, or costs than do other drugs." The authors make clear that the "hidden costs" can sometimes be recognized as related to the drug taken, though sometimes they are not apparent. The latter are the costs that tend to be ignored by those who take drugs; and this denial of the hidden costs occurs commonly with the use of illegal drugs.

Among the hidden costs of psychoactive drugs is the possibility that their use may retard or impair the individual's capacity to make meaningful relationships with persons in his environment. For youths who are heavily involved in use of such drugs, that can be as serious as the physiological effects of the drug.[50]

How implicated is the influence of the drug industry in "pushing" drugs is elaborated in what follows: On August 30, 1970, I watched a drug-education program on NBC-TV with an attention-getting title, "The Legal Pushers." I was greatly surprised to learn that the title was "for real," as the vernacular has it. The drug industry was being charged with a vast overproduction of dangerous drugs obtainable only by prescription—the amphetamines, the barbiturates, the tranquilizers—that somehow found their way to the black market. The pharmaceutical firms appearing on the program promised to cooperate with any controls imposed by the federal government. The program noted that our government was aware of the problem and would be instituting controls with respect to curbing the production of dangerous drugs such as amphetamines, the barbiturates, and the tranquilizers to the proportion needed for therapeutic purposes.

Earlier (in 1969), Dr. Sidney Cohen, then head of the Federal Division of Narcotic Addiction and Drug Abuse, had informed the House Select Committee on Crime that "the drug industry turned out an estimated 8 billion doses of amphetamines each year and that about half found their way into the black market" according to *The New York Times* of June 17, 1971. In 1970, at a symposium on drugs, reported by *The New York Times,* September 25, 1970, Dr. Sidney Cohen had urged physicians to "contribute to the diminution of the medicine chest stockpile. Many doctors save time by writing prescriptions for pills rather than really determine what is wrong with their patients."

Almost a year later, *The New York Times* (July 12, 1971) reported concern by the Food and Drug Administration and a panel of the National Academy of Sciences over two stimulant drugs in the amphetamine category, and recommended tighter controls over these drugs. One of them, Ritalin, was described as an aid in treating children, the other, Preludin, as an aid in treating adult obesity.

The recommendation was contested by the makers of the drugs, CIBA Geigy Corporation, on the ground that "reclassification would stigmatize the two products unfairly," asserting they had no evidence to justify such action.

Reclassification in the dangerous drug category was also opposed by witnesses for the Bureau of Narcotics and Dangerous Drugs and those for the Food and Drug Administration "because present law permits the same reclassification through administrative procedures. This has already been done for almost all products containing amphetamine . . ." As of this writing, the two dangerous drugs are still not reclassified, to my knowledge.

Earlier physicians in Nassau and Suffolk counties were reported to "consider a pledge to curb amphetamine prescriptions," which some authorities believe "can progress to physical addiction as serious as heroin addiction." *The New York Times* report of June 19, 1971 indicated that abuse of the amphetamines began in the 1930's when they were introduced and that since then drug companies have made available variations of amphetamines known as "pep pills . . . Today the drug industry manufactures amphetamines under some 90 brand names."

Although it is encouraging that physicians are seeking to reduce the amphetamine prescriptions, that should not reassure the American public that the availability of the highly dangerous drug in both legal and illegal markets is likely to be appreciably diminished without government control of production to conform to medical needs.

The Food and Drug Administration is beginning to be concerned with the effectiveness and contents of over-the-counter "mood drugs" —in particular, sedatives and stimulants. Senator Gaylord Nelson, chairman of the Congressional subcommittee involved, commented that "Advertising for both prescription and over-the-counter mood drugs is cleverly designed to create an unnecessary demand for them." (*The New York Times,* July 22, 1971.)

Testimony before the subcommittee revealed that "drug advertising has taken on added significance to the medical profession in that for the most part there is no other compendium of drug information than the 'Physician's Desk Reference,'" which is composed of advertisements bought at the rate of $115 per column inch. This book is given away and "used by doctors as a source of objective information."

In his opening statement before the subcommittee, Nelson said:

> There is a growing concern . . . that the increasingly close financial relationship between the drug industry and the medical profession may be contrary to the best interests of the profession and the public.[51]

The authors of *Mystification and Drug Misuse* make clear precisely what is implied in the Senator's concern and in their concern as well, namely, that "the contemporary trend of increasing prescription of psychoactive drugs is contributing to the recruitment of more and more persons into a way of life in which the regulation of personal and interpersonal processes is accomplished through the ingestion of drugs." In prescribing a drug to control or solve personal problems of living, the physician is communicating a model for "an acceptable and useful way of dealing with these problems," the authors write. ". . . Drugs do not reach the sources of the anxiety or misery, which may reside, for example, in an unhappy marriage, in the unfortunate position of the elderly in our society, or in the unsuccessful socialization of many youngsters into group settings."

> In other words, drugs do not remedy the unfavorable social and interpersonal arrangements and personal circumstances that generate anxiety or unhappiness. Through the creation of chemical barriers and through the diminishment of gross social deviance, drugs may in fact perpetuate malignant patterns and social arrangements.

Of special importance and relevance so far as teenagers and younger children are concerned is that if it were not for the availability of drugs, as I have said earlier, it would be possible to help them find

other alternatives to solutions of their problems in growing up. The
use—rather misuse—of drugs has serious consequences for the young,
particularly because they are the first generation to have been reared
under the influence of television. The full impact on youth of the new
medium has not been adequately studied. I have sensed, in talking
with adolescents, that TV has in some way prevented this generation
from experiencing in real life what they have experienced vicariously
through watching dramas, interpersonal relationships, and the solving
of problems on the television screen. Lennard and his associates add
a significant dimension to my awareness that something different has
taken place in the way today's adolescents and preteeners relate to
people in their milieu:

> Through the use of drugs such as marijuana and alcohol, the user
> feels he instantly achieves the intimacy and relatedness which ordi-
> narily come about as a result of the normal "interactional dance"
> involving mutual self-revelation, learning about the other, becoming
> sensitive and attuned to each other, and establishing a common his-
> tory of experience and points of contact. The drug user settles on
> the effect for effect's sake, bypassing involvement and social learn-
> ing.

"But," the authors add, "if human closeness is achieved only
through drugs, one does not acquire the skills necessary to achieve
these states in the absence of drugs, with the result that all that one
has learned is how to create such states through the use of drugs
. . ." Today's adolescent is overwhelmed with "informational inputs,
such as television, radio, motion pictures, newspapers," which remove him further and further from personal experience with other
human beings. "What one learns from television, for example, is how
to look like someone who has a certain position, job, or role in society.
One observes the visual appearance, the costume, the trimmings, and
the behavior. The outward form can be and is imitated, but one cannot learn through such limited interaction how to think, feel, and
relate to others in reciprocal roles; these can be learned only through
participation in the actual process of interaction itself, that is, through
practice with a variety of role partners (old, young, mother, father,
persons similar and different from oneself). Interacting with each
provides increments of knowledge about and experience with human
relationships."

The authors add that "Human depth does not come from exposure
to visual experience or the combined visual-auditory experience alone,
as, for example, in the spectator role into which television casts its
viewers . . . Watching television, then, merely provides samples from
life; it is a far cry from the real thing . . . A generation of young

people reared by such a medium finds it difficult to participate in prolonged human relationships."[52]

Just described is an experiential deprivation, a kind of self-mystification, though not consciously, that occurs in the use of psychoactive drugs such as marijuana to enhance their sensory experience, establish a sense of intimacy, and achieve friendships. However, those vanish once the effects of the drug wear off. The drug does not have the power to provide youth with the skills that are developed when the above activities are engaged in in real life and hence utilize the adolescent's own capacities. In other words, the drug acts as a kind of shadowy intermediary which, like a magician, then disappears like some fugitive, illusory image, but whose help is needed over and over again, without enhancing the adolescent's capacities to deal effectively with the problems and situations that provide continuing growth and satisfaction.

Mystification has been and continues to be used with respect to pollution both external and internal, the latter through "additives and impurities in much of what we eat, drink and breathe; even more disturbing, from the multiplicity of drugs consumed daily by many millions of Americans for other than strictly therapeutic reasons." The quotation is from an article by Peter Beaconsfield, an American surgeon now at the University of London, who expresses concern over the permanent damage that indiscriminate dosing with drugs may cause the human system in the long run.[53]

It continues as gadgets—one was recently found on the cosmetic counter of a department store: an oxygen mask for protection against pollution in the atmosphere.

In an excellent drug education program (Aug. 29, 1970) in which the viewer (or is it viewer-listener?) was asked to evaluate his understanding of eight separate statements about drugs as to whether each was true or a myth, and comparing the responses of an experts' opinion poll that included psychiatrists, psychologists, and social workers with the responses of a public opinion poll in Los Angeles county, Earl Ubell, Science Editor, CBS, introduced, summed up, and, in general, moderated the program, with an introduction and a summary.

In summing up, Ubell referred to the dilemma of drug abuse and that of blaming society, that is, racism, the draft, Vietnam, war, materialism, frustration, raising the question: "Do these explain drug abuse?" Then he asked the audience to answer this question: "Can drug abusers be cured *only* by changing society?" [Italics added.] By including the word *only,* Ubell "loaded the question," since the problem involved in the question could have been easily answered without using the word *only.* His response to the question provides a kind of mystification: "The Goal is to create better people to live in the world."

Ubell and other personnel at CBS must surely know that rehabilitation is not an either/or proposition for cure and the effectiveness of the cure. It is regrettable that Ubell, whom I have long respected and still do, should have missed an opportunity to provide clarification of a major obstacle to true understanding of the drug problem, namely, that it is not solely an individual problem, nor is it solely a societal problem. It depends on the socioeconomic status of the drug abuser, his motivation for treatment, education, personality, and other characteristics.

By July 1970, in a general indictment of the advertising industry as a whole, the criticism of Senator Frank E. Moss (D., Utah), chairman of the Senate Consumer subcommittee, that "parents as well as their children are being victimized by America's 'drug culture'," was having some effect. His request that the Federal Trade Commission study the problem was bearing fruit, as on July 27, 1970, *New York Post*'s Washington correspondent reported that the Commission had announced a study of drug advertising that was expected to pay particular attention to what Senator Moss had called "a heavy bombardment of radio and TV commercials, which seem to make the use of drugs a passport to a better life." The report also stated that according to *Advertising Age,* a trade journal, "an estimated $289 million is budgeted annually for such regional and nationwide advertising."

In this, the third decade of television and its sponsors—advertising—it is urgent that the study of drug advertising announced by the Federal Trade Commission—stimulated by Senator Moss's criticism —give special consideration to the effect on preschool children, as well as on adolescents, of the "bombardment" of radio and television commercials that, like the *pro-drug lyrics* of the rock-and-roll music industry, are especially harmful to very young children who spend so much time in front of a TV set.

## Rock and Roll and Advertising

Probably none of the modern media is so attuned to and has so influenced the very young, the adolescent, and the young adult, as rock-and-roll music. The December 1969 issue of the United Nations Bulletin includes an article that provides a graphic, albeit disturbing, picture of that influence—in particular that of the "pro-drug" lyrics. The effect on young suggestible children, already flooded with distracting stimuli they are not ready to understand, raises serious questions.

Of special pertinence is the effect of commercialism, at the root of modern advertising, in impairing the role of institutions involved in child-rearing and socialization—the family, school, religion. For too long the already powerful influence of the mass media on children has been overlooked. That influence is magnified by the commercial forces that make it possible for popular rock-and-roll songs to be heard by "hundreds of thousands of listeners." Regarding the influence of rock-and-roll records, the author, S. Taqi, states:

> Perhaps no other artistic outlet has as striking an influence on the lives of British and American youth as rock-and-roll music. Television and feature films, certainly, must also be considered influential over the young, but their potential power is somewhat diluted by the fact that they must cater simultaneously to both adult and teenage tastes in order to survive financially: TV and movies strive basically to appeal to the 18–45-year-old bracket, while the rock-and-roll music industry, in contrast, depends almost exclusively on the youth market for its profits.

The rock-and-roll product "is 100 percent aimed at the ears of teenagers and young adults (who can be anyone from about age 9 to 24 or 25)." What this means in terms of influence is that "Besides reaching hundreds of thousands of listeners via direct sales, a big record will be programmed in juke boxes all across the American and European continents, and played innumerable times on radio stations around the world. In the large cities of the United States, there is at least one station that programs rock-and-roll music" exclusively for 20 to 24 hours, pausing only to give news, the weather, and commercials. Since every rock music station will play a national hit, a single song may have a listening audience of tens of millions of pre-teeners, teenagers, and young adults.

Given such a situation, it is understandable that when the lyrics of rock-and-roll records began to make "veiled references" to the use of drugs, they had the capacity "of becoming propaganda of the highest order." The author states that the rock-and-roll industry has in recent years produced "a consistent flow of records focusing on illicit drug usage and often approving of it as a form of recreation and relaxation."

First introduced by Bob Dylan in 1965 and followed by publicity given to drug use, "psychedelic" became a "catchword for describing a state that totally overwhelmed the mind and senses." Soon psychedelic trappings followed, dresses, posters, jewelry—even nightclubs, "which tried to stun the senses with assorted visual lights combined with psychedelic music . . . With the renewed, near-frenetic general interest in pop music" brought about by the success of the Beatles, "lyrics about drugs, sex, war, became the rule rather than the exception."

Of particular relevance in assessing the influence of rock and roll is the evidence that "most of the suggestion and allusion to drug-taking" in the numerous songs the author analyzed were "doubtless intentional." He states, "I know of no serious person who believes otherwise, and it is difficult to imagine a songwriter in these times releasing one of these tunes without having a clear idea of the chords it would strike in a 'hipped' and alerted audience."

A number of factors combined to make rock and roll tremendously influential: the Beatles' attitude toward drugs was a significant one. "If they had chosen to ignore the drug trend or to remain discreet about it, the course of the trend might have been somewhat different." Also, drug use is a very real part of the rock-and-roll world and is dramatized by the frankness of many "pop" personalities in talking about drugs, together with the numerous arrests of both major and minor pop personalities.

In addition, the article notes that many of the artists believe in the "pro-drug lyrics of their songs and feel that the drug experience is a meaningful and valuable one." They raise the objection that has been raised over and over again (frequently, I find, in exactly the same words) that "there is something seriously wrong with a society that bans marijuana and at the same time allows alcoholic beverages to flow freely." A few artists, alarmed at the effects of the pro-drug songs, have attempted antidrug songs, but have met with little success, except for one record by an American group, Paul Revere and the Raiders, called "Kicks."

## Long-Range Effects of Drug-Centered Songs

The author indicates that the singers have reinforced musically their own attitudes by releasing a profusion of "drug-slanted pop songs that in themselves may have done little harm, but which appeared to be advertisements of the singers' feelings and attitudes." It is those songs that have repeatedly been shown "to have an astounding influence over the youth of the world." Moreover, it should be noted, the influence is primarily on very young children at whom rock-and-roll songs are more than ever aimed, according to Taqi, who concludes: "The end result of it all perhaps is that when, sooner or later, an urban child—who lives in the ordinary world, not in the pop world where a drug conviction can be shrugged off—is offered a marijuana cigarette or a dose of LSD, he will remember them not as something his health and hygiene teacher spoke warningly about, but as something Mick Jagger, or John Lennon, or Paul McCartney has used and enjoyed."

The examination of the effect of drug-slanted rock-and-roll songs in the U.N. article suggests that the extension of drug abuse to 8-year-olds, as Dr. Winick has indicated in "Drug Addicts Getting Younger" (referred to at the end of Chapter I), may be a result of rock-and-roll songs, which also include sex themes. These intensify the overstimulation by parents described by Winick. The implications for drug education are highly significant, and the influences, such as have been described briefly, that are supported by commercialization and advertising, need to be taken into consideration.

The author of the U.N. article makes clear that he is not condemning any songwriters or singers as "evil social beings," adding that most of the songs he used to illustrate the article are "good examples of rock-and-roll music, well written and well performed." The question he raises is "whether or not the songs should have been aimed at an audience comprised largely of children."[54]

In the spring of 1971 the Federal Communications Commission, in response to public concern, issued warnings to broadcasting stations that "they must know the meanings of lyrics of drug-associated music or face the loss of their licenses." The action has stirred up controversy that is by no means settled. Commissioner Nicholas Johnson, "the dissenter in the commission ruling, called the notice an effort to censor song lyrics . . . to determine what youth can say and hear; it is an unconstitutional action by a federal agency aimed clearly at controlling the content of speech."[55] That does not, however, do away with the problem Taqi raised in the preceding paragraph.

A *New York Times* report (April 11, 1971) states that the National Coordinating Council on Drug Abuse and Information, a private, nonprofit agency that coordinates the antidrug activities of nearly a hundred national organizations, has "joined in a suit" with two college radio stations and others against the FCC action, in the U.S. District Court in Washington. The problem involved runs through all aspects of today's mass media.

## *"Children . . . Exist for Television"*

We do, however, need studies of the effect on children of the violence, pornography, and drug use in paperbacks, magazines, movies, and television. Does that suggest that it is the society and its media of communication that need to be critically examined with respect to their influence on very young children and adolescents? Definitive answers to that question await basic studies on a national scale of the effects of more than two decades of television whose subject matter and style have been dictated by the lowest common denominator imperatives of advertising techniques to sell products and inculcate values.

Such research has long been suggested by Fredric Wertham, a psychiatrist and author of many books, among them *Dark Legend: A Study in Murder; Seduction of the Innocent; The Circle of Guilt;* and the latest, *A Sign for Cain: An Exploration of Human Violence.*[56] Especially relevant is a section in the latter book headed, "Commercial Disrespect for Human Life," in which he lists: cigarette advertising, alcohol advertising, arms advertising for the nursery, to which since 1966 should be added "drug advertising."

The research thus far on effects of mass media on children, according to Dr. Wertham, has tended "to minimize or deny any effects and also to confuse the issues." ("The Scientific Study of Mass Media Effects," *The American Journal of Psychiatry,* Vol. 119, No. 4, October 1962.) He criticizes the methods used, that is, relying on formal questionnaires filled out by the children themselves, rather than on clinical examination of the children.

Fortunately, recently a national organization representing parents and professionals that is seeking "to upgrade children's TV and the National Citizens Committee for Broadcasting, both non-profit, seeking improvement of the entire medium, are beginning to communicate directly with broadcasters and advertisers," according to *The New York Times,* June 24, 1971.

The reporter notes that Warren Braren, executive director of the latter organization, said "the truth about television is that it is not designed to make the world a better place in which to live or to give children a better chance in life," and Braren is further quoted as saying: "Despite what broadcast public relations efforts would like the public to believe, TV rarely has sought to make a meaningful positive contribution to the well-being of children. Rather, quite the reverse is true—children too often exist for television. Broadcasters are selling children as part of the television sales market."

The same criticism is applicable to the movies; the following is illustrative. *The Wall Street Journal* of August 12, 1971, includes a review of two recent movies about drug abuse under the revealing title, "The Drug Problem Romanticized." Recalling a similar treatment of gangsters while proclaiming that crime does not pay, the reviewer, Joy Gould Boyum, notes that "our ambivalent attitude toward the criminal remains . . . he appears most recently in the guise of the junkie in . . . 'The Panic in Needle Park' and 'Dusty and Sweets McGee' " and adds that although "both films are about the horrors of addiction," both films depict the junkies as "tender young lovers," undercutting "a grim surface reality." As art, she finds the films "inconsistent; as social documents, they are essentially fraudulent, and not merely because of their cloying illusions. With their lingering close-ups of bound limbs and injections, they become instructional films—how-to-do-it manuals for our time."

The film "The People Next Door," which was presented commercially and then, with minor revisions, was presented as an educational drug film, has many of the faults of the movies just described and some additional ones. The professional acting does not make up for the caricature of the two families—nor do the adolescents seem real. As for the beautiful young girl who becomes deeply involved in sexual promiscuity as well as drugs, there is nothing to help the viewer understand the "why" except on a highly superficial basis. The glamour that I found extraneous in "The Graduate" is present in full force, presumably to amuse, but it serves only to confuse.

Examination of the role of the mass media vis-à-vis today's drug-abuse problem reflects a capacity on the part of advertising—which includes far more than Madison Avenue—to be almost totally unconcerned with the harmful effects of the "products" being sold to human beings of all ages.

CHAPTER VI

# What Are Drugs? How Much Do We Know?

Few subjects arouse feelings as intense and irrational as does the topic of student drug use; in few areas is there greater tendency to distort, to perceive facts selectively, and to view with alarm. Few topics are treated with so much heat and so little light.

—KENNETH KENISTON, "Heads and Seekers: Drugs on Campus, Counter-Cultures and American Society," *The American Scholar,* Winter 1968–69 (38:1) p. 97

The state of affairs with regard to drug use described by Keniston should not be surprising, since there are few social problems of widespread interest and concern that still leave so much to be learned. A clear illustration of distortion, for example, is found in estimates of the "millions" who "have used" marijuana, without making clear what is meant by the term *who have used.* Does it include the experimenters who do not go on to use drugs regularly? Does it also include the occasional user who, after a brief period of use, has no plan to continue and leaves the drug scene, as well as the abuser? And do these statistics, which receive wide publicity in the mass media, take into consideration the number of abusers of marijuana who also, at some point, find that marijuana no longer serves any meaningful purpose? Others may, of course, take their place.

An illustration of what can be described as an escalation of the estimates of marijuana users is found in a *New York Times Magazine* article by Sam Blum. Describing an illustration of a daughter leading her father to marijuana use, he says:

But he has now become part of the most rapidly growing *estimated* statistic officially issued by the United States Government. Last October [1969] a National Institute of Mental Health pamphlet made the "conservative estimate" that about 5 million juveniles and adults had used marijuana at least once. Five months later, in March

74

[1970], another NIMH pamphlet said that "more than 8 million people have used the drug." Then, a month later, the NIMH reported to Congress that the number "conservatively was between 8 million and 12 million." In June Dr. Stanley F. Yolles, then director of NIMH, used the figure 20 million. "A standard projection curve suggests that by now one could easily find someone at NIMH willing to go for 25 or even 30."

Blum comments: "Obviously, the NIMH figures rely on some wild guesswork, but no one at all awake through the last decade can doubt the direction in which they point."

He concludes that we are now using a lot more marijuana and predicts that we are likely to use even more in the future. Such predictions, not unique to Blum, given the wide publicity that the escalation of questionable "statistics" receives in the mass media, tend to attract new experimenters. This may be one of the factors in the "progression of marijuana use to younger children," about which he expresses concern when he indicates that "This [the progression] can be used as a rigid defense against the problems of growing up," according to psychiatrists, to which Blum adds: "It is unquestionable that a certain number of children have seriously damaged their personal development by habitually turning off their problems through drugs and never learning to solve them."[57] In the second part of this chapter, some evidence on just this point is included. Part I answers the question: What Are Drugs?

However, it is important as a frame of reference within which to examine what is known, especially the research findings included in the second part of this chapter, to understand that "even so safe a drug as aspirin" has abuse potential if too much is taken at a time, and is particularly dangerous for very young children. (Aspirin for children is flavored to taste like candy.)

Some idea of how much we still have to learn about how drugs act is illustrated by the fact that although aspirin has been a "safe reliable treatment for a vast range of ills, with new uses continuing to turn up, scientists still cannot say for sure what it can and cannot do." (*The New York Times Magazine*, "Aspirin Doesn't Cure Any Disease —It is the Wonder Drug Nobody Understands," by George A. W. Boehm.) To put it in more scientific terms: "Too little is known of cellular biochemistry and physiology to permit other than an incomplete or superficial explanation of the mechanism of action of most drugs."[58] Over and over again I have asked myself this question: "What role do facts play in changing behavior?" In answering it I have had to recognize that the question was not complete. The question really at issue is "What role do facts play in changing behavior that has behind it the weight of social acceptance?"—facts largely supplied by the mass media. And in the absence of any additional hard data about drug use except that it was supposed to be increasing among younger children and also among our GI's in Vietnam, I wondered what good a presentation of some of the basic facts about drugs would do.

My dilemma was partly resolved when I decided that I would provide a brief description of the major drugs currently used for social purposes, their classification, and a brief description of major forms of treatment in this chapter.

Part II includes a summary of research findings on the hallucinogenic drugs, in particular marijuana and LSD, and also dispels some of the myths attached to heroin use. After I had convinced myself that some facts might be helpful, I recalled my feelings of confusion in watching television drug programs—even those that had educational content. They seemed rather good as I watched them, but upon rethinking what I had seen and heard, it dawned on me that the reason I was left with a confused impression was largely the result of ambivalence on the part of the media as to whether drug use and abuse were good or bad for youngsters. And I remembered all the books and articles on drugs I had read that straddled the fence or had what I call an "It depends . . . point of view," or made drug use seem exciting and glamorous.

Before providing some of the facts that I believe may be helpful to the reader, I should confess that this chapter has been the hardest one to write. In fact, there were times when I hoped it would be possible to omit it entirely, except for the part that deals with up-to-date research findings. Why? Aside from all that we do not know and are not likely to know for a long time, I have observed that facts do not seem to have too significant an influence on behavior. There are the examples of alcohol and nicotine. According to Sidney Cohen, it took "thousands of years to recognize the harm that excessive drinking could do . . . For centuries opium was not known to be addictive. Dozens of years had to pass before the Western world recognized cocaine as a dangerous agent."[59] As for the evidence that alcohol, opium, cocaine, and nicotine were harmful, it was not so much the time it took to obtain the necessary proof of harmfulness as the length of time it took for the evidence to be accepted, because profits were at stake. The most recent illustration is the reluctance of the tobacco and the related advertising industries to utilize scientific findings, and the failure of the public to heed the dangers involved in cigarette smoking. Both alcohol and tobacco continue to be sold and used, although in response to pressure, cigarette advertisements, in particular those showing young people smoking, have decreased. Whether the widespread social acceptance on the part of the mass media of marijuana is viewed as an addition to or substitute for cigarette smoking is not clear (see Chapter IV). What is clear, however, is the existence of social acceptance of the use of drugs on the part of youth and that it is sufficiently widespread not to be attributable chiefly to the personality of the drug users. That is not to deny that some adolescents are more susceptible than others to the need to experiment and use drugs. Many of the books and articles on drugs seem to have the point of view expressed by the authors of *Understanding Drug Use* that drugs are here to stay and there is little that can be done about it. Or to put it more concisely, there is a growing acceptance of the idea that *what is* is synonymous with *what should be.*

My continuing dilemma is: How to provide information that is meaningful and at the same time conveys a point of view that drug use for teenagers, preteenagers, and young adults is a waste of their creative potential as well as having the possibility of long-range effects of a harmful nature that might not show up until a later period.

In other words, how to put the emphasis on the *young* who are using drugs rather than on the *drugs* that are symptoms of the nation's unfinished business, of which peace, racism, and poverty amid affluence are the major problems requiring urgent solution. How explain that drugs are a kind of commentary on the lack of opportunity for meaningful participation in facilitating solutions, the result, among other things, of a so-called "generation gap" that I feel is partly a product of the mass media, as well as of a dehumanized and mechanized society in which applicants for employment, for example, are beginning to be interviewed by computers! And, finally, how communicate to the young, eager to take risks, an awareness of the dehumanization that occurs when drugs are used to replace the functions of consciousness by means of which human beings learn to understand and affect positively or negatively the world they live in.

Within the frame of reference used in this chapter, drugs that are currently abused may be divided into the following categories:*

1. The legal abuse of substances that are legal and have widespread cultural acceptance, for example, alcohol and cigarettes. Both number among the abusers a vast majority of adults.
2. The illegal abuse of legal drugs, for example, the amphetamines and the barbiturates. This group, too, comprises a majority of adults, though their abuse is becoming more widespread among the young.

---

* I am indebted to Seymour Rudner, Director of Research and Evaluation, Nassau County Drug Abuse and Addiction Commission, for the above classification, and for the classification that follows.

3. The illegal abuse of illegal substances such as heroin, LSD, mescaline, and marijuana. It is in this group that a majority of youths are found.

There remained a final question, namely, what kind of information to include that would have meaning for adolescents having different levels of understanding concerning drugs. The rest of the chapter is my reply.

## Part I—What Is a Drug?

"A drug is any substance which by its chemical nature alters structure or function [or both] in the living organism."[60] Keniston makes the point that "the term 'drug' covers a multitude of substances that affect human physiology and functioning," adding that there is scarcely anyone who is not "a routine user of prescribed and unprescribed psychoactive drugs, like aspirin, alcohol, sleeping pills or stimulants whose primary intended effect is to alter mood, feeling or psychological states."

He also notes that

At the present time, more than seventy percent of all prescriptions written in the United States are for psychoactive compounds—for example, tranquilizers, pain-killers and antidepressants. If we include —as we must—ethyl alcohol, caffeine and nicotine among drugs, then the American who has never "used" drugs is a statistical freak.[61]

## Classification of Drugs

The drugs widely used by youth and adults today fall into three major classifications: depressants, stimulants, and hallucinogens:

Under *depressants* are the opiates or narcotics, that is, drugs derived from opium, such as morphine and heroin. The latter are natural derivatives of opium. Methadone, a narcotic, is a synthetic opiate. Also included in this classification are alcohol, barbiturates, other sedatives, and tranquilizers.

Under *stimulants* are the amphetamines, of which there are a great many, some of which are restricted and obtainable only by prescription; others are generally available over the counter at drugstores. Cocaine is also included in this group.

Under *hallucinogens* are marijuana, LSD, and mescaline. There are other hallucinogenic drugs but less well known and less frequently used; for example, DMT and STP, as they are known. Cohen describes LSD as "probably the most powerful drug known."

The drugs referred to above are now included in the "dangerous" category, according to the Bureau of Narcotics and Dangerous Drugs. Marijuana, which is not a narcotic, has, until recently, been erroneously classified as a narcotic, with penalties as if it were one. It has recently been reclassified by the federal government as a "dangerous" drug, but has to await action by the states.

*Depressants.* Among the *depressants,* the drug most abused by ghetto youths is heroin, sometimes in combination with other drugs. It is not known to what extent the alcohol and barbiturates are also used. The latter usually are available legally from physicians by prescription. However, because of the overproduction of these drugs by the pharmaceutical industry, they are also available in the illegal market. Abuse of heroin and the barbiturates produces tolerance as well as physical and psychological dependence. By tolerance is meant that after repeated use of the same dose of a drug, the effect declines; or conversely, it is necessary to increase the dose to obtain the same effect. Withdrawal from barbiturates is dangerous and should have medical supervision. Owing to the dilute form of much of the heroin available up to the present in the United States, withdrawal from heroin is less difficult than when the available heroin was less diluted. It should also be noted that barbiturates are known to be used and abused by a significant proportion of adults—how many is difficult to estimate except by the amount produced. These drugs (that is, heroin and barbiturates) produce insensibility and/or stupor in varying degrees because of their depressant effect on the central nervous system.

*Stimulants.* This group includes drugs that *directly* stimulate the central nervous system. The most widely known is caffeine (coffee, tea, cola, and other beverages). Their effects are relatively mild and are socially acceptable. The synthetic amphetamines are abused and are dangerous, as is cocaine. In the amphetamine category is the more powerful metamphetamine or methedrine ("speed"), recognized by youthful drug abusers as highly dangerous in the slogan "Speed kills." Psychological dependence is common and can occur even with the abuse of the milder forms, such as Dexedrine, and can lead to both tolerance and psychic dependence.

It should be noted that the term dependence has been substituted by the World Health Organization for the better-known term of addiction. Drug dependence is defined as "a state of psychic or physical dependence, or both, arising in a person following administration of a drug on a periodic or continuous basis. Since there are many kinds of dependence, varying with the drug used, it is necessary to indicate the type of dependence as, for example, drug dependence of the morphine type; the drug dependence of the sedative type; . . . of the

tranquilizer type; . . . of the stimulant type . . . or of the hallucinogen type."

*Hallucinogens.* Hallucinogens are also known as psychedelics, and
are the drugs most used by middle-class youth. They are a diverse
group of drugs that "alter mood, perception, thinking and ego structure. In small doses they tend to be euphoriant; that is, to create a
feeling of happiness or well-being . . . In large amounts a wide
range of reactions is possible, depending on the hallucinogen used,
and the drug's purity and strength." These range "from horror to
ecstasy, from absence of thought to a manicky flight of ideas, from
intensification of color and depth to illusions and hallucinations, and
from minor distortions of the body image to complete loss of ego
boundaries."[62] It should be noted, however, that none of these drugs
has a constant effect, since the reactions depend on the setting in
which the drug is taken, the expectations of the drug user at the
time drugs are taken, and the mood or feelings about self at the time.
The same drug, at different times, may have different effects.

## Part II—How Much Do We Know?

In view of the focus of this book on teenagers and preteeners and the
drugs used chiefly by them, the major emphasis in this part of the
chapter is on new or generally unavailable knowledge of marijuana,
LSD, and heroin from clinicians and researchers. I am aware that a
proportion of adolescents also experiment and use, for example,
amphetamines and barbiturates. They are not new drugs, and their
misuse by adults has long been known. What is new is their availability
to adolescents, as already indicated, through overprescribing by physicians influenced by the pharmaceutical industry and through that
industry's overproduction of the drugs, which then find their way into
the illegal market. Their hazards, for adolescents, are, however, discussed.

In addition, there is much to be learned from evaluation of treatment concepts and programs. The two treatment methods that have
received the most attention and evaluation are therapeutic communities and methadone maintenance. Accordingly, a description of those
programs and pertinent evaluative material that have been made concerning them are also included.

### Heroin Addicts and Addiction

According to Alfred R. Lindesmith, Professor of Sociology, Indiana
University, an authority on narcotics, the fact that today's drug ad-

dict lives in a world separate from the larger society has served to
create "widespread ignorance of addicts and addiction," adding:

> Much popular and legislative thinking has been and is still based
> on mistaken ideas and oversimplified stereotypes disseminated by
> agencies of the mass media that are more concerned with drama and
> sensationalism than with accuracy. It is extremely difficult, even for
> specialists, to know just what is going on in the world of narcotics.

Among the areas of ignorance, Lindesmith cites the "atmosphere of
secrecy, danger and illegality" that surrounds the treatment of addicted
persons "who are presently being taken care of medically and who
do not, consequently, appear in the criminal courts." It is his view
that these individuals are often from the upper social classes "like the
addicted member of Congress who was permitted by the former head
of the Bureau of Narcotics and Dangerous Drugs to secure legal
drugs from his physician until he died." Others, he indicates, "are no
doubt members of the medical profession in which addiction is characteristically and understandably more common than in other occupational groups." I would add that some authorities note that this
is also likely to be true of nurses.

Lindesmith believes that "the systematic collection and publication"
of information about these addicts could well be of "considerable
importance in the current public debate: If some addicts can be successfully handled this way, perhaps more can." There is a basic lack
"of logic and of justice in handling upper-class addiction in one way
and lower-class addiction in another."[63]

Hans W. Mattick, Associate Director, Center for Studies in Criminal Justice, The Law School, University of Chicago, makes clear that
our knowledge of addiction and illegal drug use "is qualitative, not
quantitative, and largely impressionistic." Such quantitative knowledge as is available is information about "police activity, court actions and prisoner populations in connection with offenses against
narcotic laws," adding that "there is no valid basis for extrapolating
from 'caught' offenders against drug laws to the number of drug addicts that exist in a given jurisdiction. The drug addict is an unknown quantity in the United States."[64]

In this connection, a 1969 Drug Abuse Study sponsored by the
Maryland Commission to Study Problems of Drug Addiction and the
Maryland State Department of Mental Hygiene found that "the prob-
ability that individuals classified as drug dependent on the Psychiatric
Case Register will be unknown to the police varied sharply in accord-
ance with social and demographic characteristics of the user and the
type of drug employed: . . . females, students, housewives, those of

higher occupational status, . . . of an educational level above high school, and members of the Jewish faith," are not likely to be known to police. Others less likely "to be identified as drug abusers by police are . . . white . . . under 20 and above age 40." A major accomplishment of the study was identification of drug abusers not known to the police.[65]

It is Mattick's view that the narcotics problem in the United States is "partly a product of socialization and adjustment processes and partly a product of the public policy and enforcement procedures designed to deal with it." By socialization, he means the process by which a biological organism is developed into a human being who is adjusted to society. I would broaden the concept to include the interaction of the individual with society, that is, the smaller as well as the larger environment; such adjustment is not—or should not be—static or mechanical.

He makes clear that although it is not to be expected that "police and state's attorneys will be sociologists and psychologists, and . . . we may have been conditioned to expect something less than objective and well-rounded treatment of such a subject as drug addiction from the mass media, the time is long overdue for them to quit repeating the same old clap-trap and complicating the process of public education that is necessary in order to make a more rational attack on this serious social problem." He continues:

. . . The process of developing a biological organism into a human being who is adjusted to society is called specialization. Society is a complex series of ordered social and psychological events played out in a physical environment, a family group, an economic organization and a political structure, a legal system, a religious orientation and the preexisting communications channels of an on-going community. With so many variables entering into the socialization process it is a far greater wonder that the overwhelming majority of men become reasonably well adjusted to society than that a few do not, especially since the process is not without great difficulty during the formative years.

He adds that two broad patterns are discernible in their efforts to work out a relationship to others in the world:

Men either strive to change the outer reality or try to achieve a change in themselves in order to alter their experience of that outer reality. Those who strive to change the outer reality are the "activists," while those who strive to achieve a change in themselves are the "retreatists."

The latter "manipulate their sense perceptions in order to change the way the world and others are experienced by them . . . One sub-class of this style of life are the retreatists who manipulate their own sense perceptions by chemical means, and into this sub-class we may place the drug user."[66]

Although in some respects the above categorization of addicts seems logical, I prefer the kind of individualization of addicts—at least as a basis for treatment—that has been described in reference to the New York Academy of Medicine approach and, in particular, the approach of Chein and his associates, described below. I am in accord with Mattick's overall plan for the medical treatment of addicts, in particular his contention that it would have to be on a nation-wide scale because of the mobility and migration of addicts.

Despite evidence from sources already included, an experimental study of heroin maintenance with rehabilitative services still seems far off. A prestigious support for such a study dates back to November 1970 when an 83 page Confidential Summary of a Ford Foundation study was made available to the Mayor's Narcotics Council in New York City, to influential policy makers throughout the country and, upon request, to scholars like myself. Publication of the complete study shortly should end the attacks upon the concept of heroin maintenance by leaders in the methadone maintenance and thera-peutic community programs in light of the serious lack of treatment programs. Chein recommends "clinics as the best place for the treat-ment of addiction," adding:

And it is no ordinary medical clinic that we think of as optimal. A clinic geared to the treatment of addiction should include a wide variety of services [with a minimum of referral to other agencies], for every additional step . . . and every additional waiting period increases the likelihood of failure. The clinic should provide . . . in addition to basic medical services and a withdrawal unit, psycho-therapeutic opportunities, family casework, vocational counseling, a sheltered workshop and at least the beginnings of vocational re-training, job placement facilities, chaplains, food, financial assist-ance, a lounge where the addicts would be welcome to just come and relax, and a residential shelter. Such a clinic should be open on a 24-hour basis, . . . (but not for all services).

As a social worker, I am convinced that the concept described here is one that would make possible motivating all but the most hardened addict whose self-confidence was so minimal as to prevent his being motivated to accepting an opportunity for reeducation and rehabilita-tion.

Also recommended is the opposite of today's depersonalized clinics,

important because the addicts need acceptance as human beings before they are likely to be prepared for the treatment they need. What
the addict finds imperative initially to prepare his way to reshaping
his life is a feeling of belonging to a group that he had formerly been
excluded from and a conviction of his personal worth as a human
being entitled to and receiving respect. It would be unrealistic to expect that an addict would participate in all or even some of the available rehabilitative services, initially. The first step is to make known
these services with the assurance that these services are available to
him, but that his taking advantage of them are not conditions of his
joining the program.

Not every addict is at his lowest point and therefore need not be
viewed and treated as such. Under most programs there are participants in varying stages of need. Some are able to get jobs at the same
time and some actually are holding jobs while being served by a clinic.
The rehabilitative services are there if needed by the addict but some
are already motivated to quit their habit and want skilled assistance
in dealing with other problems.

Such a concept might seem too ideal to many because of prejudicial
attitudes toward addicts. It is realistic if we are concerned with
solutions.

Chein states that not every addict need be treated as if he were at
the "zero point of human development. There are, for instance, even
under present conditions, addicts who are capable of and who succeed in keeping their jobs. Nor do we believe that all addicts need to
be bribed with the maintenance of their addiction to avail themselves
of the clinic services; many are sincerely motivated to quit, provided
that they can be helped to cope with their other problems."[67]

Some of the services would, of necessity, have to focus on the home
environment, his family and his job. What are the chances for such a
program of rehabilitation? If minimal, let's, then, stop talking about
genuine solutions if there seems little chance for a program based on
respect for the individual addict. We must let him sense our acceptance of him before we can expect that he will be motivated to get rid
of his dependence on heroin and any other drugs he may have been
using. Without offering the opportunity, we have no way of knowing
what an addict's potential for cure may be.

## Misconceptions About Heroin Addicts

According to Dr. Henry Brill, former Vice-Chairman of the New
York State Narcotics Commission, "Leaving the literary accounts of
the pleasures and pains of addiction, it must be admitted that current
descriptions of the usual pains of withdrawal and their significance

in holding addicts in bondage have been equally exaggerated," and he adds:

> The average addict is prone to histrionics which he uses to manipulate the environment to get more drugs and to express his intolerance of frustration and even moderate discomfort but, in the long run, withdrawal pains are his most easily treated problem.

He notes that many addicts "intermittently 'kick the habit in the street' and achieve a voluntary withdrawal without benefit of medical assistance. Moreover, the 'habits' of recent years have been characteristically small and the withdrawal symptoms slight because of reduced adulterated supplies; the real problem occurs after the withdrawal is completed and the addict is back where he is in contact with others who are getting drugs, a particularly trying situation for the average case."

Many aspects of opiate addiction are still unknown, chief among them the addictive qualities of heroin.

As for the "drug dreams" of addicts, Brill observes that these exist in literature. "In real life, the addict's drug experience is contentless or content-poor, with some rare exceptions, although still very compelling. The power of the opiates over the addict is complete, but it does not reside in phantasies, illusions, dreams or hallucinations. These appear to be derived from literary sources and occupy a place in the popular imagination vastly out of proportion to their clinical prominence." He attributes the beginning of this misconception to Thomas DeQuincy's *Confessions of an English Opium Eater.*

Among the myths regarding heroin that need to be dispelled, one is that heroin causes addicts to become violent. Brill and other authorities are in agreement that opiates have "a sedative value; they hold back rather than incite aggressive action." It is generally recognized that addicts commit crimes to support their habit. Heroin does not stimulate sexual crimes. On the contrary, Brill says, "opiates have a desexualizing effect and this includes homosexual as well as heterosexual interests." Prostitution occurs to secure money for the drug.

Describing addiction as "a chronic relapsing illness or disorder," Brill notes that the addict's desire to be cured is often "overstated," and "exaggerated by some." However, he adds that it is misleading to assume that *"unless the addict cooperates and wants to be 'cured' nothing can be done for him.* In practice, addicts, like all other persons, are of at least two minds on conflictual subjects and it is sometimes possible to strengthen the addict against himself." This is a myth I have long felt is used to downgrade treatment efforts, in particular in our ghettos, popularly expressed as "Once an addict, always an addict."

One more myth needs dispelling, namely, that exposure to narcotics necessarily results in addiction. Brill discusses the fact that not all in the most heavily infected areas become addicts. In fact, he says, "only a small minority . . . become addicts."[68] I agree. However, in the eight years that have elapsed since the article under discussion was published, it seems to me that so far as New York City and the two other urban centers that have heavy concentrations of addicts, Chicago and Los Angeles, are concerned, it may be more than "a small minority." Today, in part because of the greatly increased availability of heroin and the increasing deterioration of living conditions in the ghettos in light of budget cuts for welfare, health, education, and human services generally, and a concomitant lack of treatment facilities, the proportion may have increased appreciably. (See Chapter VIII.) In Chapter VIII, the estimates of heroin addicts of the revitalized New York Narcotics Register (Department of Health) are updated.

Gaps in the knowledge of heroin has created serious social problems. There is much that we do not know, and this ignorance is compounded today because of the role that destructive social conditions play along with a tremendously increased availability of heroin. Authorities agree that heroin has no addictive effect that is universal and that many addicts use heroin on a less than regular basis and seem to be stabilized on the drug. Some are subsequently able to become free of heroin; others become addicted. There is reason to believe that among the latter, the appearance of stress or personal crisis at a time of little or no support push the individual into increased dosage and addiction.

A heroin maintenance program with sufficient rehabilitative services would fill many of the gaps in our knowledge. Equally, if not more important, such a program on a nation-wide basis would enable us to provide more effective education to the young along with basic improvement in the social conditions in our urban centers. The complexity of heroin is discussed in the following description of a treatment program that is being scrutinized and evaluated.

In an article describing some aspects of a Ghetto Addiction Treatment Center in Brooklyn, of which he is the program director, Dr. Beny R. Primm gives illustrations of the "elevation in pain threshold, which is fundamental to heroin addiction. The addict may be unaware of or oblivious to what would normally cause the most excruciating pain. Here they provide a comprehensive medical examination at the time of the first interview." The physician providing the initial medical examination "may be impressed first by the extent of self-neglect and self-destruction that are evidenced by the body being encrusted with dirt and covered with multiple scars and abscesses . . . as well as evidence of other pathological conditions." Dr. Primm notes that heroin is an exceedingly complex medical entity that will be finally characterized and conquered "only through a sophisticated, sustained, and soulful effort. A purely medical conquest will represent only a beginning . . ." There is the necessity of finding a job, money, a place to live *after* the addict has gained "the confidence and self-esteem he needs simply to pursue these necessities . . . the deep hopelessness and despair generated by the addict's sense of worthlessness are totally resistant to chemotherapy . . ." Recognition of the complexity of the etiology of heroin addiction as "a complex intangible" invulnerable to conventional chemotherapy is "the most important guideline in any therapeutic approach." Dr. Primm concludes that at their Addiction Center: "We are acutely aware of the lack of knowledge concerning heroin addiction and are resolved to fill the void."[70]

*Hallucinogens.* Marijuana is the hallucinogen most widely used by adolescents, in particular from middle-class families. It is also the hallucinogen about which there is the greatest disagreement and, hence, confusion—even among authorities. Dr. Henry Brill, while Vice-Chairman of the New York State Narcotic Commission, clarified some of the areas of confusion and disagreement: "Marijuana has been called a weak hallucinogen. It is better described as a powerful hallucinogen in dilute form."[71] (Additional data as to what is known about marijuana is included in Part II of this chapter.)

As regards marijuana, it is frequently viewed as synonymous with cannabis, although marijuana refers to the particular forms of cannabis widespread in North America. Nowlis states that "Much of the controversy about the effects of marijuana is a result of this confusion. In this country some of the vigorous opponents seem to foster this confusion by attributing to any use of marijuana the effects produced primarily by excessive use of the more potent forms of cannabis, in an attempt to preserve a strongly negative public image of marijuana."[72]

It should also be noted that the present dilute form of marijuana is sometimes mixed with other drugs, and should hashish become available, the effects of marijuana would be intensified. Current social acceptance is dependent on the present mild form of marijuana.

## Research Studies on Marijuana

A report of a study of frequent marijuana users among students at the University of California in Los Angeles (UCLA) was presented by Dr. Norman Q. Brill and Dr. Evelyn Crumpton of the Department of Psychiatry of the UCLA School of Medicine.

The results provide some support for the notion that "the frequent

student marijuana user tends to be somewhat more hostile or rebellious, to seek stimulation, to be more likely to have long-standing emotional problems and to have less respect for the law."[73]

In a report begun in the fall of 1966 on clinical observations of
regular users of marijuana for long periods in the Haight-Ashbury
area of San Francisco, Dr. Louis J. West described the results as follows: ". . . personality changes that seem to grow subtly . . . diminished drive, lessened ambition, decreased motivation, apathy,
shortened attention span . . . magical thinking, derealization, depersonalization, along with progressive loss of insight." The data were
gathered and are continuing to be gathered under conditions that Dr.
West states cannot possibly be simulated or reproduced in the laboratory, hence field studies are necessary.[74]

The findings from both studies provide significant clues to hypoth-
eses needing testing in studies with controls or at least in studies that
include careful and comprehensive investigation of the persons
studied.

A clinical study by two psychiatrists provides evidence of a link
between the onset of serious psychological difficulties and the use of
marijuana, based on thirty-eight patients between 13 and 24 years of
age. The two psychiatrists, Dr. Harold Kolansky and Dr. William T.
Moore, report that their patients did not have preexisting psychiatric
symptoms when they began smoking pot. After using marijuana, they
developed serious symptoms.[75]

These findings have been seriously questioned by Dr. Lester Grinspoon, Harvard psychiatrist and author of *Marijuana Reconsidered*
(described in Chapter VII), and by Dr. Norman E. Zinberg, one of
the authors of a study entitled: "Clinical and Psychological Effects of
Marijuana in Man." Grinspoon was critical, and rightly so, of the lack
of controls. Dr. Zinberg indicated that any "reaction to the psychological effect of drugs has to do with 'set' and 'setting' " and neither had
been explored in the reported study. What is significant is that "both
Drs. Grinspoon and Zinberg reiterated that *marijuana is not harmless*
and, in the words of Dr. Zinberg, 'nobody ever said it was.' Dr.
Grinspoon also stressed that he certainly would not want adolescents
using this or any other drug because 'adolescence is a state when under normal circumstances the ego is shaky' and drugs, including marijuana, could precipitate 'functional psychosis' in this critical develop-
mental stage."[76]

The study referred to above, of which Dr. Zinberg was one of three
authors, was a "series of pilot experiments on acute marijuana intoxication in human subjects" based on nine "naive" subjects carefully selected and eight chronic users of marijuana, also called "heavy"

users (neither term was otherwise defined). It was a laboratory study "to collect some long overdue pharmacological data."[77] Since this study is included in the references discussed below, the study is not included in this chapter, nor is it relevant. More relevant is a *New York Times Magazine* report of the study that was published a year later and its conclusion is described.

But I wish first to comment on the clinical study by Kolansky and Moore and cite their conclusions to which the Zinberg et al study has some relevance. Their conclusions are that in their patients there was a "demonstration of an interruption of normal psychological adolescent growth processes following the use of marijuana: as a consequence, the adolescent may reach chronological adulthood without achieving adult mental functioning or emotional responsiveness." The authors state that they are aware of claims that "large numbers of adolescents and young adults smoke marijuana regularly without developing symptoms or changes in academic study, but since these claims are made without the necessary accompaniment of thorough psychiatric study of each individual, they remain unsupported by scientific evidence. No judgment on the lack of development of symptoms in large, unselected populations of students or others who smoke marijuana can be made without such definitive individual psychiatric history-taking and examination."[78]

The *New York Times Magazine* report of the Zinberg and Weil article does have relevance for this chapter, notably, the conclusion, which also has a bearing on the clinic study just described. Zinberg and Weil conclude:

> The real debate about the merits or evils of marijuana ought to focus on the long-range psychiatric effects of the drug, if any. This is the main area of controversy because there are still no data at all. We have no information on the subject from our own study, and we regret the continuing lack of any good research on it. What is needed is a decent prospective study of persons—say, medical students— who are setting out to become regular marijuana users matched against a similar group not using the drug. Each group should be followed and tested seriously for 5, 10, or more years. If such a study is not organized soon, it may be too late. Marijuana use is becoming so extensive in some sections of the country that within certain age ranges, persons who do not use the drug are so unusual as to constitute what statisticians called a biased sample.[79]

A comprehensive survey of approximately fifty-odd studies, experiments, and reports entitled: "Marijuana in Man: Three Years Later," begins:

"It may soon be impossible to keep current within the rapidly growing literature. It seems propitious, therefore, to assess accomplishments in regard to marijuana's effects on man during the past 3 years, comparing these with those of the past, as well as taking inventory of what still needs to be done." As regards the latter, the author, Dr. Leo E. Hollister, notes that "looked at in its historical context, the present flurry of experimentation may have contributed less that is really new than we like to believe."

Until it was possible to obtain synthetic tetrahydrocannabinol, the active component in marijuana, and also to establish chemical techniques to quantify the content of this component, or THC, as it is usually referred to, research as to the effects of marijuana could not be precise. Three separate studies of oral doses of synthetic THC are described, one at Veterans Hospital at Palo Alto by Hollister; another at the U.S. Hospital in Lexington, where the effects of taking THC orally were compared with its effects when smoked; and the third at the University of Utah. At Lexington, it was estimated that when THC was smoked, the potency was increased three times and its affects appeared sooner but lasted a shorter time. The results of these studies and others included in the Hollister survey are difficult to generalize because of differences in the subjects studied as well as other differences. Relevant here is Hollister's view that "the clinical syndromes described for marijuana in the laboratory correspond closely to those reported by street users . . .," the most common being: "paresthesia, floating sensations, and depersonalization; weakness and relaxation; perceptual changes (visual, auditory, tactile); subjective slowing of time; flight of ideas, difficulty in thinking and loss of attention; loss of immediate memory; euphoria and silliness; sleepiness." Common symptoms not verifiable in the laboratory were claims of "increased insight and perception, as well as increased sexual desire, performance and enjoyment."

Hollister concludes from these data that laboratory experiments can be designed so that they are "highly relevant" to the effects of hallucinogenic drugs when used socially. Problems in relating the effects of social use of marijuana to laboratory research may be due to the adulterants found in street supplies such as: "oregano, *Stramonium* leaves, methamphetamine, cocaine, LSD, and allegedly heroin." Hence, reactions not explained by laboratory studies may be accounted for by the presence of other drugs. The immediate dangers, as more and more reports become available, appear to be "almost identical with those of LSD," probably because with the use of higher doses, comparable mental and emotional reactions occur. Hollister questions legal acceptance of marijuana because of the lack of many important facts.[80]

## Recent Research on LSD

The authors of *Drugs and Youth: Medical, Psychiatric and Legal Facts* (1970) include the following information about LSD in a footnote (page 65): "As this book goes to press, we learn from Dr. Cecil B. Jacobson, a geneticist at George Washington University, that a long-term and continuing study in Washington is producing strong evidence that women who have taken LSD during early pregnancy, or *even before the time of conception,* run a significantly higher risk of giving birth to abnormal babies, some with very gross deformities, than a comparable group of women who have not taken LSD."[81]

*The New York Times* describes the above study as the "first extensive, long-term study . . . a prospective study in which the mothers and fathers were followed from conception of the child, or as soon afterward as possible, through delivery" with follow-up of the offspring for two years indicating that "the rate of birth defects in children of LSD users, meaning either the mother or father or both, was 18 times as high as that of the general population."

All the volunteers had a "history of LSD ingestion before or during pregnancy." However, Dr. Cheston M. Berlin, a principal investigator in the study, indicates that "one very tough problem in ascertaining the role of LSD in congenital defects lies in sorting out LSD from a wide range of other possibly mutagenic agents used by the pregnant women. These include caffeine drinks, cyclamates, cigarettes, exposure to X-rays, poor maternal nutrition, purity of LSD used, other drugs used and history of previous illness, including hepatitis and venereal disease. All of the subjects had a history of using such multiple agents." Dr. Berlin described the group of 112 women, whose average age was 19, as a "high risk" group as far as obstetrics is concerned.

In stating that "it appears that the common denominator is LSD," he cautions that "it is hard to say that it is just LSD. We have to be extremely cautious about the conclusions we draw," adding: "The evidence, however, is incriminating." Dr. Berlin, who collaborated with Dr. Jacobson, reported that "Funds for any continued study of the volunteers had run dry. The Department of Justice, which had funded the study for two years, has not renewed the contract."

The volunteers came from backgrounds that "reflect middle- or upper-class upbringing, history of drug abuse among their parents, high divorce rates among their parents and a rather high educational level among the young people. More than half had tried drugs before they were 18 years old," Dr. Berlin reported.[82] (See also Appendix B.)

It seems to me to be indicative of a lack of interest on the part of our federal government that it fails to continue such a research project, which includes precisely the social follow-up that can only be done outside of the laboratory.

In this connection, it is significant that in concluding his survey of research, Hollister states: "The crucial clinical experiments in regard to the social questions about the possible deleterious effects from chronic use cannot be answered by laboratory experiments. These must be settled by close observation made on those who experiment on themselves." If that is true for marijuana, it is even more true for LSD, recognized as the most powerful drug of the hallucinogenic drugs described in this chapter. (See also Appendix B.)

Of special relevance for marijuana are "reports of subtle effects on the personality associated with prolonged use—loss of desire to work, loss of motivation, and loss of judgment and intellectual functions." Hollister adds:

> It may well be argued that the individual with these manifestations may have developed them in the absence of drug use, but available evidence does not allow this assertion. In view of the fact that many drug users are recruited from segments of our youth most favored with intelligence and opportunity, the future loss of a large number of these individuals from productive society could be of considerable social consequence.[83]

These reports may well prove to be the kind of evidence that may clarify the debates that since 1969 have been arousing interest or concern over legalization of marijuana.

## Treatment of the Heroin Addict

The concept of the "therapeutic community" and that of "methadone maintenance" have in common that both treatment methods consider the addict as a sick person, but there are differences in the way each views the sickness. The supporters of methadone maintenance programs assume that the addict has a "metabolic deficiency disease derived from heroin addiction that requires replacement with a drug." The therapeutic community concept considers the addict as an immature individual, with personality deficiencies that necessitate what is often described as "total character" change. Given the frame of reference of this book, it is my observation that neither treatment method takes into consideration the socioeconomic and cultural milieu from which a majority of addicts come and the social, educational, and economic effects of racism. It is for that reason that some

black and Puerto Rican community groups have expressed distrust
of both types of therapy.

## What Is Methadone Maintenance?

Methadone is a synthetic narcotic with pain-killing effects similar to
those of morphine. Methadone has been used in heroin withdrawal
(detoxification is the medical term). However, if detoxification is the
only treatment, chronic, long-term addicts usually return to heroin.
It was the failure of methadone detoxification as a "cure" that led to
the development of methadone maintenance programs through the
pioneering teamwork of Dr. Vincent P. Dole and Dr. Marie Nyswan-
der at Rockefeller University. Their work resulted in the discovery
in 1964–65 that "methadone given in carefully stabilized daily doses
destroys heroin hunger and creates a blockade against any effect from
using morphine or heroin or any other morphine derivative." It was
following "a careful pilot study" on six patients that the clinical investigation was transferred to what is now the Bernstein Institute of
the Beth Israel Medical Center and Harlem Hospital Center where
they launched "a large-scale clinical investigation. Not only did they
evaluate their own work but their research has been subjected to an
outside evaluation" by Columbia [University School of Public Health
and Administrative Medicine] and an advisory committee of experts."[84]

Since methadone is a narcotic, and like heroin, is addictive, with
withdrawal symptoms and craving for another dose of the drug, it has
to be administered on a regular and continuing basis, beginning daily
and then, for some addicts, reduced to three days a week as their
progress warrants. It is administered orally in Tang or in tablet form.
When taken intravenously, both drugs cause a euphoric sensation
called a "high," although heroin is said to produce a much more sat-
isfying high. One might then ask, why substitute methadone for heroin
if the two drugs are so similar? The major reason is that when dispensed as part of a treatment or research program, methadone is
legal, whereas heroin is illegal. But then the question can be raised:
Why can't heroin be dispensed legally to known addicts? The proponents of methadone maintenance reply that methadone is a longer-
acting narcotic (12 to 48 hours, depending on the dose), compared
to heroin, which must be taken every four to six hours. Thus, methadone is much more practical for use in a long-term treatment program.

The Dole-Nyswander experimental program, after the pilot program referred to earlier, began in 1965 for persons addicted to

heroin for at least five years who had no evidence of *major* psychiatric or medical problems, and who had failed in other treatment programs. [Italics added.] This resulted in a largely older (25 years plus) and predominantly white patient group. Social rehabilitation was centered largely on employment, primarily outside of the treatment program itself.

In September 1969, Dr. Frances R. Gearing, head of the Columbia group evaluating the methadone program, released a report that "indicated that 92 percent of those addicts in the program for 36 months were employed or in school and that of the 2,205 total admissions to the program, the overall drop-out rate was 18 percent. These impressive statistics are paired with data that indicate a substantial decrease in the number of arrests of program participants, compared with their record prior to entering the program. Also, it is claimed that addiction to other drugs is limited: Fewer than 10 percent of those on methadone maintenance are found to be using amphetamines or barbiturates, and only 11 percent abuse alcohol." Finally, Dr. Gearing reports that "none of the patients who remained on the methadone maintenance program has become readdicted to heroin."

The June 1970 issue of the Bulletin of the Health Policy Advisory Center (PAC) questions drawing inferences from a "biased sample to all addicts." For example, they cite Dr. Harvey Gollance of the Beth Israel program: "Methadone administered daily in controlled doses would allow 80 percent of all addicts now on the streets to begin self-supporting, normal lives." Also cited is Dr. Dole's claim that "maintained addicts would have an 80 percent chance of becoming acceptable citizens." Serious reservations have been voiced by the publication of such claims "because of selective admissions procedures and the voluntary character of the methadone maintenance program. Success may be directly related to the population of addicts who have been primary program participants. They have tended to be male, white, and over 25 years of age." Certainly this would not be called a representative sample of New York addicts. It should also be noted that since this is a voluntary program, there is a self-screening process. It would be difficult to generalize from such a biased sample to the entire population of addicts. The criticism is somewhat tempered by the notation in the publication that "other programs have reported success with less highly selected groups."

Criticism of the independent evaluation reports is also based on evidence that the data collection "was not independent of the program." When Dr. Gearing, the physician primarily responsible for the evaluation, was asked if her committee went out and got its own information, she replied: "The evaluation committee did not go out . . . We got our reports of arrests in two places, both from the program and the police . . . Initially, we did the employer business . . . we have not done it for some time." Apparently, the primary evaluation data are "the unit directors' reports compiled from counselors' reports, all of whom are employees in the program." In addition, the "employment data are not so impressive in absolute numbers. Only 88 patients have been in the program for three years, so, if 92 percent are employed, only 80 patients are employed after three years in the program. Moreover, some of these patients are employed by the program itself; Dr. Gearing refuses to say how many. Thirdly, some doubt is cast on the statement that none of the patients remaining on the program has become readdicted to heroin, since detailed data about heroin usage have not been reported."

The PAC criticism concludes that methadone clearly has a place in the "treatment of the opiate addicts, probably more because of its legality than because of its 'medicinal' qualities. Few would deny the utility of methadone for narcotic detoxification, but many would question the implications of chronic methadone maintenance. Methadone maintenance alone appears to be no more than an attempt at a simple medical fix to a complex social, political, and psychological program. Social and psychological rehabilitation is also necessary."[85]

Some ghetto leaders believe methadone should be used exclusively with addicts over 40 and not with youth. According to federal guidelines, the lowest limit is 18. In my view, 18 is still too young for this kind of treatment, because it assumes that adolescents cannot be helped to "kick the habit." Also, the Dole-Nyswander program approach does not have any ancillary services, such as stimulating addicts to function more effectively in the communities. Their objective is to help the addict with methadone alone. Other programs have used group psychotherapy, educational and job placement services.

Also, without knowledge of the social characteristics of the addicts in the program it is difficult to assess the results.

In the summer of 1970 a *New York Times* story reported that the methadone-only program was undergoing crucial tests. Two experiments had begun. One was being conducted by Dr. Harold Trigg of the Morris Bernstein Institute (Beth Israel Hospital), in which 1,700 patients were undergoing methadone treatment. The methadone-only experiment was to be limited to 100. The other test was taking place at the New York City methadone treatment unit. At the Addiction Treatment and Research Center in the Bedford-Stuyvesant section of Brooklyn, Dr. Primm said he was conducting his experiment completely independently of the Beth Israel test and was experimenting with other ways of using methadone. Both tests are being watched closely by the advocates of methadone as well as by those who have complained that it does little more than satiate the addict without coping with the psychological causes of his addiction. Also, advocates and critics alike are watching to see whether methadone only will be sufficient to rehabilitate addicts who were never really a part of productive society. One of the chief criticisms of methadone maintenance is that it promises no permanent abstinence from drugs. The newspaper article (July 26, 1970) stated that if tests showed a dramatic decrease in crime and if a large number were able to get jobs outside of the program and could take the first steps toward leading productive lives without help from counselors, this would result in a revaluation of ancillary services.

If the tests are unsuccessful and addicts given methadone only leave the experiment or "continue to abuse drugs and indulge in antisocial behavior . . . it will tend to reinforce the belief that methadone maintenance by itself is not enough—especially when given to addicts who have really never been a part of productive society—and that addicts will need other forms of assistance before they cease to be a drain on the city's resources."

*The New York Times* cites the proponents of the Dole-Nyswander technique as saying that although never acknowledging that ancillary services are totally unnecessary, they hold that it is futile to deal with the psychological aspects of addiction. Psychotherapy, the Dole-Nyswander proponents say, "has proved a long, costly, and often disappointing process."

In contrast, Dr. Primm, director of the Addiction Research and Treatment Center, believes the major function of methadone is to allay the fear of withdrawal, but that one standard dosage will not do it. In fact, he has been experimenting with a group of fifty-eight "exemplary" patients to see how little actually is needed to do the job. In spite of systematic reduction of dosages, he has found that "exemplary" patients continued exemplary, using drugs less than do other patients, and showing up more regularly for their various appointments. "One still needs about 100 milligrams a day; about half are at 50 or less, and some are doing well on only 10 or 20 milligrams a day."[86] But the most significant innovation is that eighteen patients have voluntarily stopped taking methadone entirely while remaining in the program and continuing their therapy and other activities. In a "Methadone Information Brochure" for addicts, the concept of eventual withdrawal from methadone is included.

Those results, if confirmed, contradict Dr. Dole's theory that heroin addiction produces permanent metabolic changes in the body that result in an equally permanent drug hunger. The theory holds that methadone satisfies the drug hunger but that because the hunger is permanent, methadone maintenance also must be permanent. See

Appendix for more recent evaluation of methadone maintenance treatment programs.

## Therapeutic Communities

Although ostensibly there is *a* concept of treatment called the "therapeutic community," in actuality there are a number of varying versions. Nevertheless, drug-related therapeutic communities have a similar view of the addict as an individual who is immature and emotionally disabled by lacks in his early development within the family and is suffering from a chronic disorder. Given that view—essentially a psychiatric view that gives little consideration to the impact of the environment on the family and indirectly and directly on the addict —the programs are described as having an openness, honesty, and warmth of interpersonal relationships that dispel some of the alienation and loneliness of modern society that addicts feel strongly—possibly more strongly because of their lack of self-confidence and, hence, poor self-image. Not surprising in light of what is known about the early histories of drug addicts. The community or "house" represents the addict's family.

Treatment focuses on the emotions that drive the addict to drugs, of which heroin is one, and a major one. It is achieved through three methods: encounter group therapy; a highly structured community; and a reward-punishment system based on behavioral psychology. Encounter groups vary in size, frequently having some twelve to fifteen participants. They single out one individual, whom the group then questions and accuses ruthlessly by means of violent verbal confrontation. The addict is caught in his lies and manipulations and is forced to face his present behavior. The long-range goal is to bring about a cure of the addict's character disorder.

Not all addicts can take that kind of confrontation. Therapeutic communities generally are in agreement that the highest proportion of dropouts occurs in the first three months. There has been criticism from black and Puerto Rican addicts; from the former, that encounter sessions and the treatment generally are basically middle-class and have little applicability to the communities to which they will be returning; from Puerto Ricans, the criticism is that encounter sessions are almost invariably carried out in English, putting Spanish-speaking persons at a disadvantage.

A major criticism of the therapeutic community approach that I have heard and that I share, is its emphasis upon drug addiction as an individual problem rather than as a symptom of social as well as individual pathology. In that connection, it is of interest that David

Deitch, an ex-addict from Synanon, the first therapeutic community, who directed the city's Daytop program on Staten Island, was forced to resign from Daytop "when he proposed that addicts be trained to return to their communities as political activists."[87]

Some therapeutic communities now include professionals as well as ex-addicts at the administrative level as has been the practice, in the Nassau County Drug Abuse and Addiction Commission since its inception with major responsibility for treatment in the hands of professional staff. In addition, flexibility is being manifested by beginning early to prepare the addicts for "reentry," and not necessarily to accept as failures addicts who leave (or "split," as it is called) before the end of their treatment; also, to permit some splitees to find therapy in groups to which they can relate or to return to the therapeutic community for completion of the treatment without feeling that such addicts necessarily "contaminate" the other addicts in the house. Other therapeutic communities are finding that some addicts may be rehabilitated more readily on an outpatient basis by group psychotherapy for themselves in conjunction with separate therapy for their families.

The most innovative therapeutic communities are those utilizing nearby community colleges, even high schools, to provide early possibilities for addicts to complete their education, to feel more comfortable in maintaining contact with nonaddict peers, to be able to have vocational training outside, as well as to have outside institutions provide education and training in the "community" or "house." This has been the policy at Topic House in Nassau County for some years now and has worked well. It is beginning to be clear that there is no one type of heroin addict.

In addition to therapeutic communities, group therapy, rap sessions, storefront counseling of parents and relatives of drug addicts as well as group psychotherapy and sensitivity groups for drug abusers of so-called "soft" drugs, suburban community groups have inaugurated a number of independent treatment centers, sometimes with state funding, sometimes with community funding. Halfway houses are beginning to be available in some areas for youthful drug abusers. Experimentation is going on but it is growing "wild" rather than becoming part of a large blueprint on the basis of which each experiment could conceivably make a contribution to our understanding of the problem and, hence, shed light on solutions.

The views of the black community regarding treatment were forthrightly expressed by a spokesman at the March, 1971, annual meeting of the American Orthopsychiatric Association. The spokesman for one of the first—and apparently still one of the few—black-community-controlled drug rehabilitation programs told the press conference that dealing with the drug problem is not a job for experts, but for the community itself, according to a report on her talk in the March 1971 issue of "Drugs and Drug Abuse Education" Newsletter.

"It seems drug addiction only became a national hazard when it seeped into Scarsdale," said Mrs. Martha Davis, representing the United Harlem Drug Fighters. "We've had trouble with drugs for the last 30 years and lost as many kids through drug abuse as we have lost in Vietnam. We are actually wiping out a generation of people. This makes us take the radical and militant attitude we do. We think we are the experts because we are living with it and that our race is primarily affected by it."

Her group is "community-based and community-controlled, so automatically the 'system' doesn't approve of it," she continued. Her organization, which treats primarily adolescents 9 to 16 years old, took over two floors in a Harlem hospital last summer and kept them until the hospital and city negotiated for other facilities.

While obviously community groups such as the one just referred to can accomplish much that other treatment programs may not be able to duplicate, I have to conclude this all too brief discussion of the therapeutic community treatment programs by predicting that these constitute token efforts unless combined with community pressure from the ghettos to improve conditions in these neighborhoods, e.g., education, housing, employment, and in addition to take the profits out of heroin if the spread of heroin addiction is to be stopped. In 1963, the New York Academy of medicine stated unequivocally:

> However much sociological and psychological factors influence a numerical increase in addicts, only by supply can addiction spread . . . Failure to recognize the economic factor or to misjudge and disparage its potential can only misguide away from the most promising approach to stopping the spread on a mass scale. For removal of profit is the easiest and most effective way by mass action to check and stamp out the spread of illicit traffic.

In an editorial, "Death and Disability in Drug Addiction and Abuse," Brill dispels a highly prevalent myth of special importance in light of the increasing number of adolescents and preteeners who are abusing dangerous drugs, including heroin. I refer to the myth that heroin addiction does not involve serious medical problems. Whereas the two papers upon which the editorial is based deal with heroin addiction, Brill discusses the implications for the abuse of drugs that is widespread today. Based on two papers cited below, Brill notes that "Heroin addiction emerges more clearly than ever in these papers as a life-threatening and deeply hazardous existence with a long series of gruesome complications such as tetanus, malaria, cardiorespiratory failure, pulmonary fibrosis, and endocarditis as well as the better known 'overdose'."

In view of the length of time it has taken to establish clearly the above-mentioned medical complications, Brill raises the question of how long it will be before we may expect "a reasonably full evaluation of the direct and indirect medical consequences of the many new forms of drug abuse that are now developing." He refers to the hazards of LSD, which have already been covered in this chapter; the need for research in long-term use of marijuana is included in Chapter VII. To these should be added the amphetamines, the barbiturates, and the tranquilizers.

As Brill indicates in his conclusion, since abuse is widespread in the population, it is important that studies such as the two discussed be undertaken in order to provide "an early warning system to identify adverse ractions as soon as possible." He further notes that "the proportion of all drug abusers who finally develop some type of chronic disability may prove to be considerable." Although this still remains to be determined, "it is abundantly clear that the increasing misuse and abuse of drugs pose grave medical as well as social problems to today's society."[88]

What is lacking, so far as treatment programs are concerned, is evaluation. There is no consensus even as to what such evaluation should include. The July 1971 issue of the *World Health Chronicle* includes a section on "Prevention and Treatment of Drug Dependence," part of which is devoted to a remarkably clear and simple description of the criteria of evaluation of programs that can serve as a model:

> Adequate evaluation requires an explicit identification of goals, a classification of cases that will permit the establishment of valid comparison groups, and the use of standardized methods of data collection. The evaluation of therapeutic outcome requires the collection of data on the psychic state, on the frequency of criminal activity and recourse to drugs, and on other factors relating to social and economic adjustment. Such evaluation cannot be as precise as many laboratory procedures, since full control of the social and psychic variables that may influence the overall outcome may be impossible; nevertheless, such work as has been done indicates that valuable data can be obtained that, in addition to providing a guide to the further development of services, may resolve some of the controversies about the management of drug dependence.

CHAPTER VII

# *The Marijuana Controversy—*
# *Legalization?*

There needs to be a greater awareness and acceptance by the community at large of the doctrine that drugs and medicine are not ordinary articles to be abused at will . . . The pharmacist has long preached this dogma because from his expert training he knows the problem of drug abuse will continue to be aggravated by the wide availability of drugs of all kinds and by the indifferent social attitude to their proper use.

> —J. C. BLOOMFIELD, Chairman, Committee on Drug Dependence, Pharmaceutical Society of Great Britain, "The Abuse of Drugs and its Prevention: The Pharmacist's Role," *Royal Society of Health Journal,* July–August 1970. (Vol. 90, No. 4)

It is clear that pressure for legalization of marijuana is related to the widespread use of the drug among middle-class youth. So far as I have been able to trace this, the increased availability of marijuana paralleled campus dissent, with the increased use beginning to be apparent sometime during the latter part of 1968. By 1969 the controversy, or movement over legalization, depending upon one's point of view, became public. This was noticeable in the number of position papers that were being prepared and made public by a variety of organizations interested in and concerned with youth and the use of drugs, both voluntary and public. The increased use of marijuana was particularly noticeable among middle-class high-school as well as college students in the suburbs and in middle-class communities in metropolitan areas. The use, or at least experimentation with marijuana had also made itself felt among upper-class youths, some from our most prominent families.

In the early stages of the movement, legalization was confused with the need to decrease the legal penalties for use and to seek ways to undo the harm caused by the erroneous classification of marijuana as a narcotic.

Adults found themselves on opposing sides of the controversy, differing with other adults as well as with their children, and the discussions that took place in communities where an atmosphere of hysterical emotionalism prevailed were hardly conducive to rational discussion. That marijuana had been used by adolescents and younger children in the ghettos of our large cities, with no outcry about its illegal status, is a measure of the degree to which marijuana had become a predominantly middle-class problem. Besides, by that time, heroin was the major "drug"; heroin was the enemy.

As of the present writing (September 1971), the controversy over legalization continues with little evidence of added clarification of just what this will mean. And in the proposals presented there is insufficient consideration of the problems that are likely to arise if, after legalization has taken place, research findings provide evidence that marijuana smoking is harmful for adolescents and younger children.

In examining the differing views—mostly pro, either because those opposed are not writing or are not being published, I have been taken aback at times by the attitude of some of those who favor legalization, whose attitude implies not only acceptance but legitimization of drug use. Illustrative are the following excerpts from *Understanding Drug Use:*

> The world is what it is and *how* it is, and the young will continue to use drugs, no matter what adults do . . . Clearly, the young can misuse their drugs and damage themselves; they often need some kind of help—attention and alternatives, connections to one another and adults, but giving that help is a tricky process. We write with the young looking over our shoulders, aware that they need adult help but that they must be protected from adults' zeal, for the "help" they receive can be more damaging to them than the drugs they use.

> Not all those who use drugs are problems—nor do they have them. *Hard* narcotics are always destructive and their spread is frightening, but the *soft* drugs—marijuana, the psychedelics—are more variable. *Some* of them give *some* trouble to *some* adolescents at *some* times; but not always, not even most of the time. For better or worse, drugs have become as American as violence or cherry pie, a normal part of the adolescent world.

Surely the young deserve something more from us than the defeatist attitude that whatever is, must be; and if they do, nevertheless, go down the road to drug use, so what! After all, only *some* of them will be destroyed!

The authors go on to correctly place much of the responsibility for youth's escapism and rebellion on their adult models.

*Imitation.* Paradoxically, what appears to parents and the young as rebellion is in part an imitation of adults: a grotesque, unconscious mimicking of their patterns of distraction and escape. Liquor, coffee, tobacco, pills—we all know what it takes to keep adults going day after day in lives that would be intolerable without artificial relief. The young continually see adults treating their own symptoms, changing their own moods. Adults rarely confront the underlying causes of their discomfort. We rarely take hold of our lives and make them lovely or truly livable. If we do not use drugs, we use bridge and television. We distract ourselves and deal obliquely with pain; we repress or avoid the parts of the self demanding attention.[89]

If many adults do indeed lead lives of futile diversions to escape understanding themselves, are we being truly loving to the young to imply that, of course, they must do the same? Surely this must be interpreted by the young as our indifference. Moreover, just as all the young are not attracted to drugs, so all adults, the author's comments notwithstanding, are not leading meaningless lives.

What is involved in the above excerpts from *Understanding Drug Use* is a somewhat repetitive pattern throughout much of the book, with the exception of the latter half, that seems to imply advocacy, both directly and indirectly, and that amounts to legitimization of drug use.

Some other illustrations of the legitimization of drug use, with or without overt support for legalization, are to be found in Charles Reich's *The Greening of America,* in William Burroughs' novels, in the poems of Allen Ginsberg, among others.

Public airing of the debate or controversy, depending upon your point of view, began in 1969, when a number of committees—state, county, and federal—began to hold hearings on the subject. It was at such a hearing, on legalization, that Margaret Mead made the headlines: "Dr. Mead Calls Marijuana Ban Worse Than Drug": "We are damaging our country," she said, "our laws and the relations between young and old by its prohibition. This is far more dangerous than any overuse." She said marijuana was safe "unless taken in harmful and excessive amounts, but anything used to excess is harmful." Indicative of an acceptance of drugs was her interview with reporters in which she favored psychotropic drugs, such as tranquilizers, stimulants, hypnotics, and anti-depressants "to help man cope with the stress and anxiety of modern life . . . We should not have to face unnecessary anxiety when a pill would relieve the tension."[90]

A similar attitude is discernible in the statement of Canon Walter

Dennis, Jr., of the Cathedral of St. John the Divine in New York City when, in his sermon on Oct. 11, 1970 he urged "that the smoking of marijuana be legalized, and the thousands of people now in jail for using it be granted immediate amnesty."

> It would be preferable to find ways toward fantasy and rapture which do not rely on chemicals and external stimulants, just as it would be nice to induce gaiety and relaxation without martinis and bourbon, *but that would require a very different society from the one we have today.* [Italics added.]

In a discussion later, Canon Dennis stated, according to *The New York Times,* that "the main factor that had crystallized his outrage about 'discriminatory' marijuana laws was the growing body of medical knowledge indicating that the drug was harmless," to which he added: "I believe that until there is compelling medical evidence that marijuana is harmful, its use should not be illegal."

I was not and am not now aware of any "growing body of medical knowledge" that indicated the harmlessness of marijuana. Also implied in the earlier part of his rationale is the same kind of pessimism regarding the potential of human beings to cope with problems without drugs, as well as failure to make clear that the church is interested in and willing to participate in social change. To accept resorting to a chemical whenever a problem arises tends to deprecate the individual's own capacity to handle stress, thereby preventing youngsters from gaining confidence and ego strength—something an adolescent needs.

In an article contributed by Gore Vidal to *The New York Times* of September 21, 1970, and published under the heading: "Drugs: Case for Legalizing Marijuana," the writer advocated a plan for legalization that would simply make "all drugs available and sell them at cost. Label each drug with a precise description of what effect—good and bad—the drug will have on whoever takes it."

Aside from the failure to realize that the effect of any drug varies with the age and susceptibility of the individual to the particular contents of a drug, which varies at different periods of life, the suggestion is more in the nature of a flip and cynical attitude toward a serious problem than a genuine contribution to its solution. Nor does he seem to be aware of the relationship between the use of drugs and the effect on youth of the erosion of the quality of American life. This tends to undermine the confidence of youth in adult society to solve our current major problems. This lack of awareness is also apparent in Dr. Mead's statement and that of Canon Dennis.

Erich Goode, Associate Professor of Sociology at the State University of New York, Stony Brook, presented his views in a piece entitled, "Turning On for Fun" in *The New York Times* of January 9, 1971. Belittling the experts and their explanations for the use of drugs on the part of youth, he said:

"The simple fact is, marijuana is fun to smoke. Now, this will seem like a flabby justification to anyone who has not allowed himself much pleasure in the past forty years, but hedonism carries a great deal of weight in some circles." It is "increasingly a recreational drug," he continued, for "larger and larger numbers of young (and not so young) people." He indicated that *"this will not disappear, and it will not abate; drug 'education' campaigns are doomed to failure."* He minimizes claims about the hazards of marijuana and concludes: *". . . as far as the long-term organic damage is concerned, the worst that could be said is that there is as yet no proof of it. So the question has to be: Why not smoke grass?"* [Italics added.]

Goode's cavalier dismissal of the dangers of marijuana pending proof positive has a serious fallacy. It is like the arguments in favor of continuing nuclear testing in the atmosphere when the danger was foreseen and predicted by atomic scientists. Accordingly, attempts were made to prevent further testing. The prediction of harm by the atomic scientists was based on evidence that was belittled at the time by our government, which offered the same argument that proof of harm could not be demonstrated in advance of testing. Of what value is scientific knowledge that permits prediction if then we are asked to wait until the prediction comes true—in the case of marijuana, until long-term effects that are harmful become apparent? Such a view as that of Goode reflects an antihuman philosophy and a laissez-faire policy that has resulted in the degree of pollution we now find in our environment. Scientists in our industries must surely have had the knowledge to predict the pollution. It was not *profitable* for the industries to utilize that scientific knowledge.

As a social scientist, Goode should know how long it takes to obtain the kind of evidence needed for us to know whether marijuana is or is not harmful—at least a generation, especially since up to the present we have had too little knowledge of the characteristics of those adolescents who smoke marijuana even to set up a control group for purposes of study, or to obtain prospective data from new users. In addition, there is a growing concern over the possible effects of marijuana by inhaling for longer periods than in the case of cigarettes. And, finally, have we forgotten the tragedies of the premature acceptance of the "harmlessness" of the drug Thalidomide? It seems necessary to reiterate that it is standard pharmacological practice— *when it is not overlooked*—that "the hazards of a drug must be fully evaluated and its safety established before it is released for general use," according to Dr. Henry Brill, as cited earlier.

A letter by Dr. Ralph N. Wharton, Assistant Professor of Psychiatry, College of Physicians and Surgeons, Columbia University, in response to Goode's article, was published in *The New York Times* of January 15, 1971. Dr. Wharton was critical of Goode's knowledge, attitude, and reasoning:

> A physician who gives medicines carefully weighs the risks versus benefits in estimating a therapeutic ratio. There is no drug without risk—whether it be penicillin, morphine, or aspirin. The data on the risk with marijuana remain unknown because it is a complex of chemicals of variable potency depending on where the marijuana is grown and prepared.
>
> . . . As a doctor who has done extensive medical research with psychoactive drugs and knows the extent of the unknowns, I feel it a matter of conscience that those who publicly ignore the dangers be publicly reminded of our and their ignorance.

Part of a *Life* magazine feature on marijuana was an article by Dr. James L. Goddard: "Should it be Legalized?" in which facts essential for serious examination of the legalization controversy were presented within a frame of reference that makes clear the gap between what we know and what we need to know. According to Dr. Goddard, formerly director of our Food and Drug Administration, "Man has used marijuana both socially and medicinally for several thousands of years and yet today there is little scientific knowledge of its dangers or its merits. In spite of our lack of knowledge, an estimated 12 million Americans have used the drug in recent years. Now we are in a near crisis caused by ignorance and the blanket of misinformation which governmental agencies have used to cover their ineptitudes."

We now know that marijuana is not a narcotic, although our federal laws (and most state laws) have erroneously defined it as such. Recently, marijuana has been reclassified as a dangerous drug, with the other hallucinogens, for example, LSD and mescaline. However, each state has to change its laws if it wishes to do so. (See also Appendix C.)

According to Dr. Goddard, among the effects of marijuana that the user seeks are: "A state of relaxation, an enhancement of sensory stimuli . . . an apparent expansion of time, and a *dispelling of the problems of the day*," [Italics added.] That, he indicates, may be the chief danger of the drug, occurring as a result of chronic or regular use of marijuana, and would be particularly harmful to an adolescent or even a younger person who might become psychologically dependent upon marijuana instead of coping with problems of his everyday life.

Dr. Goddard lists the questions under investigation by the National Institute of Mental Health: Does long-term usage of marijuana have harmful effects? Does it affect the reproductive processes? What type of treatment will be most effective in rehabilitating marijuana users? What conditions favor continuation of marijuana use as opposed to moving to hard drugs? What kinds of educational approaches are most effective in reducing misuse? Does marijuana affect human chromosomes?

According to Dr. Goddard, answers to some of the above questions would be forthcoming within a matter of months (though it was not indicated which questions), and Dr. Stanley Yolles, then director of NIMH, was credited with indicating that "within two or three years, most of what we need to know will be available."

That is an unrealistic estimate of the time needed: *first,* because middle-class youths have not been using marijuana long enough for a study to be made of the chronic and long-term effects of the drug, and *second,* because such a study would require follow-up over a long period of time. And it is precisely the data from such a study with a sufficiently large and representative sample that would be needed to support legalization, if legalization is to be based on scientific evidence—rather than pressure from middle-class America—adults as well as youth.

Some sense of that pressure is apparent in Dr. Goddard's preface to his statement that he was not recommending legalization, namely, that what he was suggesting "would not satisfy those who seek to legalize it." He makes clear that the present legislation is a "mixture of bad science and poor understanding of the role of law as a deterrent force," and he added: "They are unenforceable, excessively severe, scientifically incorrect and revealing of our ignorance of human behavior." He cites the arguments of those urging legalization: that the laws are not enforceable; that the use of marijuana is a private act and does not harm society; and that marijuana is less a danger than alcohol.

Examining critically the logic of those arguments, he refutes them as follows: "(1) . . . laws may have a deterrent effect; (2) although marijuana is a private act, it has the potential to cause harm to society, specifically the possibility that with marijuana more freely available and more widely used by adolescents who have not learned to cope with the problems of daily life, marijuana could become a societal problem," to which he adds: "Our inability to keep cigarettes away from minors [also alcohol] should serve as a reminder that we would not be able to keep marijuana out of their hands . . . I believe that if alcohol and tobacco were not already legal, we might very well decide *not* to legalize them—knowing what we now know."

As to Dr. Goddard's underestimation of the amount of time required for answers, I am sure he is aware of this, and I can only interpret his statement and the one attributed to Dr. Yolles as indices of an increase in general support for legalization.

Support for legalization is not always based on awareness of the kind of facts we need to assess long-term effects on teenagers and pre-teeners of smoking marijuana. This inference is based on analysis of the two books by advocates of legalization, one by an attorney, John Kaplan, *Marijuana, the New Prohibition,* published in 1970, the other by psychiatrist Lester Grinspoon, *Marijuana Reconsidered,* published in 1971, as well as Dr. Grinspoon's article in *Scientific American* of December 1969. I have also examined feature articles such as that in *Newsweek* of September 7, 1970: "Marijuana: Is It Time for a Change in Our Laws?," in which questions such as the following are raised: "Is marijuana all that harmful?," and which includes such statements as: "The August issue of a New England medical journal called the *Massachusetts Physician* recommended editorially that grass be placed under the same controls as alcohol." This is balanced by evidence of the known hazards of marijuana, the most serious of which is "the amotivational syndrome among grass smokers—passivity, concentration on present pleasure rather than future goals or hard work, a lack of ambition and initiative," presented by one of several marijuana opponents.

The *Newsweek* article provides the core of the missing ingredient as to knowledge of long-term use of marijuana, and states very clearly and succinctly that *"pot smoking hasn't been widespread in this country long enough to study the effects of a lifetime of turning on; presumably that will take another generation."* [Italics added.]

It is further reported in the *Newsweek* article that "nonenforcement of the laws seems to be spreading," with "free zones" where marijuana can be smoked and distributed almost openly, for example, college campuses . . . "Probably the freest zone of all is the middle-class living room." Dr. Graham Blaine, chief of psychiatric services at Harvard asks: "Why don't we turn our backs on it [marijuana] and concentrate on LSD, heroin and amphetamines—maybe marijuana just might go away? There is so much confusion on the effects that we ought to have a moratorium before we start looking into the laws."

I am in complete agreement with Dr. Blaine as regards this suggestion. As a matter of fact, I am convinced, though I cannot prove it scientifically, that if the availability of marijuana had not greatly increased in the two-year period between 1966 and the latter part of 1968 coincidental with increased dissent on college campuses, marijuana might have remained a fad at the college level. Earlier marijuana had spread to a few of the prestigious high schools in urban centers through friends or siblings from the colleges. The increased availability of the drug together with growing social acceptance reflected in the mass media resulted in widespread use among younger and impressionable adolescents whose immaturity and lack of judgment made them easy targets for the latest fad: the use of drugs. Once a sufficiently large group of young people were using marijuana, the contagion spread, thanks to present-day youth's conformity within the peer group.

It should be noted that in the three works mentioned earlier I analyzed chiefly those portions that are most relevant to legalization. Dr. Grinspoon's *Scientific American* article of December 1969: Marijuana: The Anxieties of Our Time," which seems to be reflected in "Attitudes Toward Marijuana," includes a brief summary at the beginning:

> There is considerable evidence that the drug is a comparatively mild intoxicant. Its current notoriety raises questions about the motivation of those who use it and those who seek to punish them.

He is referring to the fact that "Social prejudices may well be a factor in the 'public alarm' on the part of the older generation, which sees marijuana as a symbol of the alienation of the young." He believes that marijuana is condemned by adults, "whereas alcohol is accepted because it lubricates the wheels of commerce and catalyzes social intercourse." And this constitutes an obstacle to legalization.

In citing what he calls "the most detailed clinical account" of marijuana, namely, the 1934 description by the noted New York psychiatrist Walter Bromberg of the psychic effects of marijuana, Grinspoon indicates that in some persons "the hedonistic desire may develop into a dependency." He raises the question as to whether such a use of the drug (marijuana) can be considered abuse. "Although the dangers of alcohol, even of social drinking, are well established, social drinking is not considered abuse in the United States," adding that "the dangers of the use of marijuana, on the other hand, have not yet been clearly determined."

Again, I have to point out that it was, is, and should be generally recognized that we do not have definitive evidence of the harmfulness or harmlessness of marijuana. It is likely to be a generation or possibly more before we will know for certain one way or the other, *providing* we begin a comprehensive study in the near future.

In *Marijuana Reconsidered,* Grinspoon states: "It is quite true that among the hundreds and hundreds of papers dealing with cannabis [marijuana] there is relatively little methodologically sound research. Yet out of this vast collection of largely unsystematic recordings emerges a very strong impression that *no amount of research is likely to prove that cannabis is as dangerous as alcohol and tobacco."* [Italics added.] In this excerpt from the concluding section and the one that follows, it becomes clear he is convinced that no additional research is needed to support legalization:

> It is reasonably well established that cannabis causes no tissue damage. It does not lead to psychoses *de novo,* and the evidence that it promotes personality deterioration is quite unconvincing, particularly in the forms and dosages used in the United States today. Although it is clear that much more must and will be learned about the derivatives of this fascinating plant, it is not so clear what specifically needs to be learned before we are ready to embark on a more reasoned approach to the social use of marijuana.

Although Kaplan's book *Marijuana: The New Prohibition* reflects some of the same urgency regarding the need for legalization, he is much more explicit in describing his plans for legalization—three different models. In contrast to Grinspoon, he points up an area in which research is needed, making reference to the fact that the argument regarding legalization "has in great part shifted to the major area of uncertainty regarding marijuana—the chronic effects of the drug." He states that unlike the acute effects, chronic effects are "very difficult to determine," indicating some of the difficulties, such as making allowances for differences in socioeconomic status, psychiatric instability, and the effects of other drugs, as well as the fact that marijuana use among the middle class has not yet continued long enough to have produced a representative sample of chronic users; and finally, the fact that "the use of marijuana is illegal makes it extremely difficult if not impossible to do the kind of follow-up studies of users that would be most valuable."

In that respect, I am in agreement with Kaplan. The essence of my plan—to remove the punitive effects of the law from the user—is precisely to make it possible to obtain the kinds of social data essential to assess the effects of long-term marijuana use. This would require detailed social data from the participants in any study such as the one described at the end of this chapter.

Kaplan mentions that "Abusive use of marijuana undeniably does exist, resulting in the individual's elevating its use to a position of primary importance in his life and creating a strong psychological need for the drug. When this occurs in the very young it can be a very serious interference with normal development."

Kaplan also notes that for some users "dependence on marijuana can be a very serious problem . . . ," not so much for adults as for school-age children for whom dependence on marijuana "may lead to missed homework assignments, failure in schoolwork, and a general attitude that one can escape the difficult problems of growing up by retreat into a drug-induced euphoria." The latter effect may be most significant in permitting the adolescent to avoid the problems of growth, thereby leaving him "half grown up and without sufficient 'coping mechanisms'" with which to respond to the "challenges of maturity." (This is comparable to the findings reported in Chapter VI, Part II.)

That he does not give sufficient weight to the seriousness of the long-term hazards in his stress on legalization may be explained by his concern for the criminalization of the adult as well as of youth by present laws and also his view that "The real problem today is recognizing the difference between prescribing for the welfare of an individual patient and recommending a course of action for society. For the latter purpose, we must weigh not only the benefits of suppressing marijuana use, but the social costs of attempting to do so as well. It would seem that to make these social costs bearable marijuana would have to be vastly more harmful to the user than the evidence indicates."

It is apparent that my frame of reference in viewing the matter of legalization of marijuana is focused largely on its actual and potential harm for the young, whereas the emphasis on the part of both authors is largely on the social costs. In that respect I differ with both Kaplan and Grinspoon. It seems to me that in a truly humanistic and democratic society the needs of both individuals—and the society would not require the kind of decision to which Kaplan refers in the citation above.

It is apparent that my frame of reference in examining the merits of the legalization proposals of both Kaplan and Grinspoon differs from theirs. They seem to be more focused on the harm caused by present laws, whereas I am concerned about the effects of a psychoactive drug in impairing the capacity of *youth* to solve problems as well as the potential harm of chronic use of marijuana. If *only* adults were using marijuana it is hardly likely that the controversy would arouse so much emotionalism. It is because my knowledge of many health problems leads me to believe that although for adults, it *may* not be serious not to await findings as to the cumulative effects of chronic use over a long period of time, that idea carries the potential of serious implications for youthful users of marijuana, an increasing number of whom are in the 8-to-12 age group, not only socially as has already been indicated, but physiologically as well.

As regards the arguments for complete legalization of marijuana, it is relevant to point out that the well-known authority on drugs, Alfred R. Lindesmith, suggests that the marijuana user be treated as the alcoholic user, and if he is to be punished, it should be by means of fines only. In addition, he points out that "the more conservative reformer can call attention to the fact that, outside of a few Asian and African countries, the use of this substance is everywhere disapproved of and subject to legal restrictions." He notes the possibility that legal restraints exercise a deterrent effect, without which there might be increased use of marijuana.

I am in complete agreement with his view that:

> A comprehensive, impartial public inquiry into the matter, based on the assumption that marijuana is *not* the same as heroin, might help to bring about a more sober and rational approach to an indulgence which merits some concern but which is far less serious than is presently suggested by the harsh inflexibility of current laws.[91]

In the article, "Marijuana in Man: Three Years Later," a comprehensive review of research findings, the author, Leo Hollister, considers the question of whether marijuana should be legalized. He finds the arguments for legalization elaborated in detail and "superficially quite convincing," but adds: "A distinction should be made between legalization and making something 'less illegal' as by eliminating penalties for possession for personal use." Citing the differences between the present control of alcohol and what this would mean for marijuana, he states: "No one feels constrained to watch over every field of corn, but would anyone dare leave a field of marijuana unguarded?" He notes that whereas no one can produce a potable alcoholic beverage easily from that corn, "the weed comes ready to use." Hollister is in agreement with most of those who believe that criminal law "is not a suitable means to control the problem of drug abuse," having failed in practically every instance. Accordingly, he adds that what may be more "immediately appropriate would be to eliminate penalties for possession of marijuana for personal use," rather than to establish a new body of laws that might prove as difficult to enforce as the laws we now have. As regards the social use of marijuana, Hollister points out that "We lack many important facts for making a proper judgment about the desirability or undesirability of accepting this drug into our culture," indicating some important "but not fully answered questions," most of which are not answerable by "laboratory experiments."

That makes the inclusion of research that takes into account the social characteristics of the users especially significant. As regards the question: Should marijuana be equated with alcohol as a social drug? his reply is of special significance:

> In terms of its low acute toxicity, as compared with alcohol, marijuana would appear preferable . . . On the other hand, the degree

of impairment from casual or continued use seems to be about equal for either drug *assuming that equivalent mind-altering doses are taken.*

The author adds that the dose of marijuana is extremely difficult to gauge in its presently available form, whereas that of alcoholic beverages is most precise. He suggests that this problem might be resolved by using synthetic THC (the active component of marijuana). Other problems are the differences between a dose by smoking and an oral dose. However, in his view, "the greatest problem is the assumption that marijuana would supplant alcoholic beverages for a great number of people," adding that "past history suggests that the drug would simply be added" to the use of alcohol by many and that many might use marijuana who would not ordinarily take any social drug.

In view of the urgent need for data concerning current use of marijuana on a sufficiently large and representative sample of our youth population, I recommend that penalties for personal use be dropped as soon as possible. It will be impossible to involve a sufficiently large sample, with a control group of teenagers and preteeners, so long as it is a crime to smoke marijuana. Following the removal of penalties it would be necessary to obtain support—financial and philosophical—through private foundations. Youth must be involved in this plan from the very beginning. The plan will require the holding of a series of local conferences to culminate in a national conference to publicize the objectives of the research and to stimulate the reexamination of all the various forms of drug abuse by adults as well as youth, with particular emphasis on the narcotics and the highly dangerous drugs, such as LSD, the amphetamines, and barbiturates.

I can best sum up the opposing views of persons who are authorities in the field of drugs, such as Hollister, for example, and Lindesmith, compared with authorities such as the authors of the two books on legalization, by stating that such decisions as those involved in the marijuana controversy are not likely to be made on the basis of the facts alone, but also on individuals' philosophical views, their views about people, in this instance concerning those who have the most to gain and conversely the most to lose—namely, the adolescent and preteenage users. In a drug-drenched culture such as ours, which is only now beginning to take a hard look at the role that drugs have assumed—taking away from human beings responsibility for solving problems in daily living through reliance on themselves and the help of other human beings—it will be necessary to dispel the myth in the question Earl Ubell raised in his otherwise effective drug education program (see Chapter V): It is not possible to create better people except by making a better world. The myth in all forms of current methods of drug control lies in the failure to take into account the social roots as well as the dependence that occurs merely through repetition of the behavior.

"So long as one lives, change is possible; but the longer such behavior is continued the more it permeates other consonant modes . . . Personality change follows change in behavior. Since we are what we do, if we want to change what we are we must begin by changing what we do, must undertake a new mode of action . . ." (From "How People Change," by Allen Wheelis in *Commentary,* May 1969).

Specifically, that means that merely a focus on drug use—a symptom of a serious erosion, in particular of the nonmaterial aspects of life—will not accomplish the objectives I have outlined above. The involvement of youth in the research to obtain the data regarding marijuana needs to be followed up by involving them in all of the major aspects of American life from which they have up to now been excluded. The young know what adults seem not to know, namely, that they are no longer seen as necessary for the functioning of the nation. That must change if we are to expect solutions to today's problems of drug abuse.

A question that underlies abuse of all drugs is "how and why has our society become so dependent on drugs and what are the factors that are causally related," and finally "what needs to be changed so that this dependence on drugs can be changed to dependence on self and other human beings?"

It is necessary for adults to realize, as Keniston has so aptly described, that "Drug use can indeed be a kind of cop-out, not from perversity or laziness, but simply because there seems to be no other alternative. Student drug use is indeed a commentary upon American society, but it is above all an indirect criticism of our society's inability to offer the young exciting, honorable and effective ways of using their intelligence and idealism to reform our society."[92]

# CHAPTER VIII

# *If We Want Solutions . . .*

If by some miracle, we could acquire new leadership in the White House, if that leadership recognized the evils of our society and mobilized to deal with them, we could not only separate the mass of the youth, the blacks, the Chicanos and the other discontented from the desperadoes but deprive the desperadoes themselves of the self-righteousness that sustains them. I imagine an America with a new Roosevelt, with a President who said—and made us feel he meant it—"We are embarking on a 10-year crusade to wipe out racism, illiteracy, pollution, urban blight and war. To do so we are withdrawing from Vietnam and cutting our military down to bare-bones size. Come and help us build a new and shining America." Think of what we could do with the zeal that now moves some of our best youth to destruction.

—I. F. Stone's Bi-Weekly, September 21, 1970

Political and historical events do not have a direct, one-to-one relationship with drug use; the war in Vietnam does not *cause* students to smoke marijuana or experiment with LSD. But the political climate of the past few years has created a negative view of the possibility of meaningful involvement within the established institutions of the society, at the same time that it has convinced many students that society is in desperate need of reform. This climate of opinion in turn contributes to the assumption that if meaning, excitement and dignity are to be found in the world, they must be found within one's own cranium.

—Kenneth Keniston, "Heads and Seekers." *American Scholar,* Winter 1968–69, p. 112

In the implementation of the two excerpts cited above lie genuine solutions to today's drug abuse problems. In essence, both Stone and Keniston point to the evils and lacks in twentieth-century American society that are causally related to drug abuse, but not in a direct one-to-one relationship that is readily discernible. On the basis of a thorough investigation that has delayed very considerably the preparation of this book, I have come to the conclusion that our

115

Administration in Washington is in possession of the facts—and much more not available to me—that I have included in this chapter, but for reasons that I can only infer, the Administration has not seen fit to utilize this knowledge in finding solutions. The facts, my interpretation, and the knowledge upon which my inferences are based are included in this chapter, supplemented by additional data in the Appendix.

The basic premises underlying today's drug-control methods need challenging. They are illogical, abysmally ineffective, wasteful, and contribute to, rather than resolve, the very serious problems with which the nation in the 1970's is confronted with respect to the problems of drug abuse and addiction. The mythology that surrounds the current investment in a punitive method of control is a major roadblock in finding solutions. Another roadblock arises out of failing to understand that drug abuse is a symptom of the crisis our society is facing and, hence, to pay attention concurrently to the changes that must be made if the young are to feel that the credibility gap is being bridged between what is professed and what is done. The results of national opinion polls suggest that the nation as a whole is aware of the crisis and of our major social problems, ending the war in Vietnam, problems in the economy, drugs, putting an end to racism, poverty, and injustice, but feels helpless and apathetic about doing anything about them.

Waste is embedded in our present law-enforcement method of control. Moreover it weighs most heavily and punitively upon the user of drugs instead of upon the purveyors of drugs—the profiteers and their protectors, some of whom are identifiable, if not identified —this becomes apparent in any critical examination of the problems of heroin addiction on the part of our GI's in Vietnam.

I am referring to the need to examine critically the punitive approach that views drug abuse and addiction as a crime. It is particularly inappropriate in a society that stimulates the use of drugs as a solution to practically all of life's problems and approves of their use. For too long there has been a need to consider other approaches. This has been largely discouraged by a blackout that prevented Americans from learning about the methods of control in use in Western Europe, particularly in England. And when information about the English plan has been presented in our press, it has been largely inaccurate until recently.

The importance of considering other approaches is urgent because of the resurgence of heroin addiction in the post-World War II period, and the greatest increase has been among the young—the school dropouts and the high-school graduates in the ghetto slums who could find no jobs. Because of lack of money these youths are driven to pushing and to criminal behavior in order to support their addiction. This accounts for the epidemic nature of today's heroin addiction spreading in our urban ghettos. It is significant that the New York Academy of Medicine in its three successive reports—1955, 1963, and 1965, which stress the need to decriminalize the treatment of addicts, emphasizes the powerful influence of the huge profits in the illegal traffic in heroin as a major factor in the spread of addiction.

Notwithstanding, there seems little reflection of the above reports documenting the need to rethink current methods of control. Instead, in 1970 John Ingersoll, Director of the Bureau of Narcotics and Dangerous Drugs of the Department of Justice, stated:

> If we are going to eradicate drug abuse thoroughly and permanently, the beginning will be in the family. To talk only in terms of eliminating the illicit drug supply is a shortsighted approach; *we need a long-range program that will eliminate demand as well.* [Italics added.] We must restore and emphasize some established and tested values— family cohesiveness and intrafamily communication—the best possibilities for getting the message to youth . . .[93]

The persistence of the myth that demand creates supply suggests lack of awareness of the role that availability plays in the traffic of illegal drugs, heroin in particular. Dr. Dana L. Farnsworth, Director, University Health Services, Harvard University, describes the role of availability thus:

> But one of the main reasons for the drug abuse problem is simply that drugs are so readily available. Once the idea of drug-taking became fashionable, a huge potential market was established, and the suppliers were quick to grasp their opportunity. This easy accessibility means that there is a deceptively easy answer to all the adolescent's problems, defy society and authority, identify with his peer group, imagine he is discovering his true self, and enjoy the thrill of a dangerous and unknown experience, all at once.[94]

The New York Academy of Medicine, in its Report on Drug Addiction II, July 1963, explaining the importance of viewing heroin addiction as a medical and public health problem, points out that "The more vigorous the police action against illicit traffic, with the consequently greater risk, the higher the price of the product and the greater the profit. Finally, another development has added a particularly vile and despicable, but again highly profitable note to an already sordid and contemptible racket. Cultivation of juveniles and teenagers or pandering to their inclinations opens a 'dream' market of lifetime sales."

In that connection, Chein and his associates provide another graphic explanation of how availability in the ghettos creates demand: ". . . In the case of narcotics, one needs access; and there are many reasons why access should be, by far, easiest in large cities. Organized crime, of which illegal traffic in narcotics is but one aspect, is itself a phenomenon of large cities. Until a sufficiently large corps of salesmen can be built up out of *entrapped addicts,* the basic personnel of the business must be drawn from otherwise criminal elements of the population, and these would be conspicuous if they invaded areas radically different from their normal habitats." [Italics added.]

The authors also note that:

> Insofar as the bribery and connivance of some law enforcement officers is a necessary condition of the maintenance of the traffic, the problems of making the right contacts must be enormously complicated as the number of independent law enforcement agencies involved increases. In addition, the illegal traffic in narcotics confronts many difficulties as is and hence has especially much to gain from a potentially concentrated market; it does not, so to speak, need the extra headaches of a dispersed market.[95]

The persistence of the myth that demand creates availability overlooks the implicating role of the adult society from high-powered advertising of the mass media in glamorizing the drug scene, as well as the more subtle advertising of the pharmaceutical industry, described in Chapter V. As for the role of the family in education, such education is well-nigh impossible in a punitive atmosphere, especially when the impact of law penalizes the user disproportionately in comparison with the illegal trafficker-profiteer. Nor is the family immune from the blandishments of advertising about the role of drugs to make life more bearable. On that point, Dr. Farnsworth has said: "When purveyors and users are treated with equal severity, the true purpose of legal penalties becomes obscured."

In view of the crime attributed to heroin addicts, of the fact that drugs have become the leading cause of death for people between the ages of 15 and 35, as noted earlier, and of the increasing number of preteenagers who are addicted to heroin, the question arises as to why there has been no public outcry or debate about an alternative approach to the heroin problem, as there has been, for example, in the case of marijuana.

One of the few recent public references to the need for consideration of an alternative method of control is an editorial in *The Wall Street Journal* in July 7, 1971, "New Priorities on Drugs," which stresses precisely the point made by the New York Academy of Medicine in 1963 with respect to the effect of successful law-enforcement efforts in limiting supplies. And, even more surprising in view of the blackout that has surrounded the control efforts in England, the editorial describes briefly their plan:

> The British long ago foresaw the futility of an approach to the problem that depends so heavily on "prohibition." It has traditionally permitted heroin addicts to register with the authorities and obtain enough drugs to maintain their habits from doctors or hospitals at a very low cost.

Although the report mentions some abuse on the part of doctors, it is clear that it has been "relatively minor. Hard drugs and the associated crime are relatively small worries in Britain. The only conclusion can be that Britain has never allowed itself to become a highly profitable market for hard drugs, unlike the U.S." The editorial ends on a hopeful note, but in my view finding a more rational approach will require considerable pressure and far more public debate than has been the case as we approach the middle of 1972.

Discussion of a control plan as an alternative to the present law enforcement dates back to the post-World War II period when the increased prevalence of heroin addiction stimulated interest in European methods of heroin control. This led to the appointment of a Joint Committee of members of the American Bar Association and the American Medical Association in 1955–56. In his introduction to the interim and final reports of this Joint Committee, Alfred Lindesmith described the two basic needs of the joint enterprise "involving not only the cooperation of the legal and medical professions but also that of the police and of all other interested groups and individuals" in *"full and free investigation and full and free discussion."*[96] [Italics added.] That kind of cooperative reevaluation of our drug program is precisely what has been lacking in the intervening period, and what must be restored if we are to resolve the perplexing and costly problem of heroin addiction and drug abuse generally.

## Intimidation of the Medical Profession by the Then Narcotics Division of the Treasury Department

In order to understand our present impasse in the control of heroin, it will be useful to examine the recent past history. With the Harrison Narcotic Act of 1914, narcotics previously available readily and legally over the counter came under strict government control. Physicians became the authorized prescribers of narcotics for medical purposes and were responsible for their ultimate use. This revenue law to control the drug traffic was not intended to interfere with medical treatment of addicts. The Act does not apply "to the dispensing . . . of narcotic drugs to a patient by a registered physician . . . in the course of his professional practice, and where said drugs are dispensed or administered to the patient for legitimate medical purposes . . ."[97] In fact,

> The system of using clinics to prescribe narcotics was tried in the United States between 1919 and 1923, when more than forty clinics were in operation under the auspices of state and local governments. Many of these survived the threat of federal prosecution for only a short time, and eventually the Treasury Department succeeded in closing all of them. We have, nevertheless, documented evidence that at least one clinic, which lasted for a period of about four years, proved highly successful in treating addicts . . ."[98]

Nevertheless, physicians began to be indicted through the Narcotics Division, although most were following accepted medical precepts.

In the Linder case (1925) the Supreme Court made clear that the physician alone had responsibility to decide whether to give drugs to his addict patients. . . . This reinforced the physician's authority. Notwithstanding, from 1914 to 1938, 25,000 physicians were arraigned, 3,000 received jail sentences, and 20,000 were fined. The results of this harassment of doctors by the Narcotics Bureau was that physicians were intimidated and withdrew, never permitting the addict to reapproach them. The addicts, thus abandoned to their addiction, were driven to the illicit traffic to satisfy their compulsive needs for the drug.[99]

A question arises as to whether the intimidation of the medical profession and the resultant criminalization of heroin addicts were not to some extent further influenced by the changed character of the groups addicted to heroin, since a majority of the post-World War II addicts were found in the ghettos of our large cities. It will be recalled that heroin addiction on the part of high-school students in New York City ghettos during the 1950's went unnoticed so far as solutions were concerned, despite the deliberations of commissions and committees and the passage of a law requiring instruction in narcotics in state schools. Nothing came of either the deliberations or of the law. In that connection, it should be noted that it was "only when marijuana became desegregated and upwardly mobile" that there was an increase in societal attentiveness."[100] Moreover, pressure for legalization of marijuana has not been accompanied by a comparable public debate regarding the need to decriminalize the drug addict.

Signs indicate that the issue of "legalizing heroin" is beginning to receive some attention. In March 1971, hearings were initiated by New York State Senators and Assemblymen sitting as the Subcommittee on Narcotic Drugs of the Temporary State Commission to

Evaluate the Drug Laws. The "official subject of these hearings was methadone and other drugs used in heroin addiction, with the emphasis on the cost and expansion plans of the various methadone maintenance programs" now being operated in New York City. Neither the methadone maintenance programs nor treatment programs for heroin addicts are available for the vast majority of addicts.

Against estimates of 100,000, which "many knowledgeable people think is now approaching 200,000 heroin addicts, the estimates of the number in any kind of treatment program are as follows: Methadone maintenance, about 5,000; therapeutic communities, roughly 2,500; day care, out-patient counseling centers, etc., about another 2,000."

Including "the entire 5,500 people in the state Narcotic Addiction Control Commission's 17 treatment centers around the state on the grounds that a heavy majority are from the city, the total adds up to about 15,000 people and fits well with a recent estimate of the city Addiction Services Agency Commissioner Graham S. Finney of about 10,000 in the city alone (10 percent of his estimate of the 100,000 city addicts.)"[101]

Kenneth Brodney, the reporter, who is very knowledgeable regarding the city's drug problems, notes that "a generous estimate of the waiting lists for all the treatment programs in town will probably not yield more than another 10,000" and that adds up to about 25,000 now in or seeking treatment.

Subsequently, Commissioner Finney's estimate of 100,000 New York City heroin addicts was updated to between 300,000 to 400,000 by the revitalized Narcotics Register of the New York Department of Health. Initiated in 1963 but starved for funds until recently by "the reluctance of various agencies to send in reports," this register is unique in that it "does not just compile treatment cases, . . . nor just arrest cases . . . It gets reports of any contact with a narcotics abuser from more than 400 sources, including treatment programs, hospitals, the police, the courts, other city agencies, and private industrial and business firms. A long-reluctant Board of Education has finally promised to start reporting users among students, but many private physicians continue to drag their feet, usually on the grounds of worry about stigmatizing their patients or getting them into trouble with the law." The two researchers are Sherman Patrick, Director of the Narcotics Register, and his superior, Dr. Lawrence Bergner, Assistant Commissioner for Research and Professional Training in the New York Department of Health. Confidentiality of the identity of the narcotics abusers is "zealously guarded" by the Register and has the added protection of the city Health Code.[102]

The revised estimates should encourage Joseph L. Galiber, chairman of the state subcommittee on Narcotic Drugs, to examine critically "every aspect of the heroin problem, including 'the British clinics with their controlled distribution of heroin, and inquire whether this approach or something like it deserves a try in New York.' This has been a subject for conversation for years, but Galiber seemed to be pursuing it with new vigor and to be looking for, among other things, the possible reaction of the black community."

To revert to Brodney's March 25 *Village Voice* story, the reporter cites Bronx Senator Robert Garcia as "planning to introduce a bill during the current session authorizing 'a pilot project for the legal dispensation of heroin—heroin maintenance under strict medical supervision, and with all the other services an addict needs.' " Garcia had visited England for nine days in February and although admitting that the problem was very different because of the disparity in the number of heroin addicts, "what impressed him most was the British system's ability to reach the addict by giving him legal heroin. Then they can try to deal with his problem," Garcia said, usually reducing his habit, using methadone or any other method. Garcia also indicated that the British give their addicts heroin in soluble pills of uniform quality and strength, also a supply of sterile plastic syringes, thereby cutting down on infections.

The article notes that a bill is already before the legislature, though it does not specify a pilot project. Instead it would authorize "clinics to dispense heroin to registered addicts only and only under medical supervision at the clinics.

The reporter adds:

> What the politicians are beginning to grapple with, and what many doctors are still less inclined to look at, is the basic confusion of two very different social processes with very different outcomes, although the two often overlap. These are the creation of addicts and the creation of criminals.

A recent hearing provides more realistic estimates of the number of heroin addicts in treatment in New York City. Of the 300,000 addicts it is estimated that some 25,000 to 30,000 are in treatment. (*The Village Voice,* Kenneth Brodney. March 2, 1972.)

## The Returning GI's

The urgency of dealing with the epidemic growth of ghetto addicts is now further intensified by a new factor, the returning Vietnam veteran addict. It has been variously estimated that between 5 and 15 percent of GI's in Vietnam are taking heroin. Until recently the public has remained ignorant of the facts thanks to the attempt by the military to mask and minimize them, even to the extent of discharging such men into civilian life without treatment.

How can such a shocking state of affairs have developed, that the young men we sent to fight an immoral and unpopular war should be doubly punished by being exposed to heavy heroin traffic, directly aimed at them in South Vietnam? A recent television program attempted to answer that question.

An ABC-TV documentary, "Heroes and Heroin," presented August 21, 1971, provides significant evidence of American involvement in the availability early in 1970 of increasing quantities of heroin processed in Thailand and Hongkong and "sent back across the Saigon docks into Vietnam." The opium, according to an ABC news correspondent, Howard Tuckner, who has covered the story of drug use by the military for the past five years, is grown in remote parts of Laos, Burma, and Thailand, known as the Golden Triangle and "is smuggled into Saigon's airport at Tan San Ut by stewardesses on Air Vietnam by pilots of the Royal Laotian Air Force and by Laos crews aboard the planes of Air America." Tuckner adds that "both planes and crew are bought and paid for by the United States Central Intelligence Agency." The heroin "was openly sold and used in the back alleys of Saigon and on the streets around American military bases." The reporter makes clear that heroin was available "anywhere anyone wanted it . . ." A medical corpsman reported that the "worst heroin found was about 91 percent. The purity is such that you can smoke it, snort it, eat it."

A psychiatrist, Captain Brian Joseph, Head of Detoxification, Canh Tho, South Vietnam, is cited as stating that the GI's constitute a susceptible population and that life in Vietnam has much in common with the ghetto existence, especially that of the early 1950's in Harlem, when "narcotics addiction swept through like a plague." Life in the barracks, he says, provides little privacy; there is a great deal of boredom together with harassment by the noncommissioned officer comparable to that suffered by the Negro at the hands of the white policeman. Those aspects of the GI life, coupled with the lack of emotional satisfaction and the message from the media that "if you have a problem, take a pill," were cited as factors conducive to heroin use. Unfortunately, warnings by medical officers that drug use was spreading were "either ignored or suppressed by their military superiors . . . The military's recognition of the growing drug problem led to the creation of an amnesty program . . ." According to Tuckner, despite denial by military authorities, "there appears to have been a change in the interpretation and implementation of the ground rules." Dr. Robert Landeen, "former head of program at 101st . . . Asst. Division Psychiatrist," describes this as a redefinition of amnesty; "instead of giving us total amnesty, they're now making it something different, called legal amnesty. So in effect, they're having people come in with the understanding that they won't be prosecuted in any way, and yet once they're in the program, then they find out that . . . there may be little prosecutions in various forms, such as change in their pro pay, change in their duty assignment."

Some idea of the cover-up on the part of American and South Vietnam authorities as regards the heroin problem may be gained from the difficulty ABC encountered in interviewing Dr. Landeen, who was known to be critical of the drug program, which was serious in the 101st Airborne . . . despite the crackdown. "When ABC's Steve Bell tried to discover the story by talking to doctors and drug suppression teams," he found, after going through official channels, that when he arrived at the 101st Division, Dr. Landeen had been asked to visit fire bases . . . and was kept away from the base for almost two days. When, however, it became clear that Bell was in fact going to interview Dr. Landeen, the latter was spoken to by his PIO officer, who tried to coach him as to what he should say and also to subtly intimidate. Dr. Landeen commented, "I was told that perhaps I didn't have all the facts, that maybe I didn't understand it. I felt that this was a very subtle form of intimidation. I was told to be very careful what I said because this could be perhaps dangerous to the Army as well as myself."

In addition, "raids" to which ABC reporters were exposed were in places in which opium "has been smoked more or less openly for years" but not by GI's. During a search on a merchant ship in the Da Nang harbor, where "much of the heroin that comes into this area arrives by sea," one customs official "told the captain not to worry, that the search was for the benefit of television cameras, and that perhaps the captain himself should suggest which staterooms the customs officials and Navy personnel would search . . ."

Frank Reynolds concludes that "from all we have learned about the drug problem, we find that ignorance of its dangers and refusal to recognize its threat were principal factors in allowing the situation to get out of control. We find those two elements continuing to prevail even today. In the military, the Veterans Administration and among some of the judiciary we find that false optimism and cover-up continue." The summary ends with approval of the Administration's program that some addicts will have to be maintained on methadone, with psychiatric help to decriminalize their addiction "provided it is made available throughout the United States to any drug addict anywhere." The program's view is that a "voluntary program simply will not work," hence "there should be some form of compulsory treatment for all addicts; . . . there is nothing voluntary about their need."

Accordingly, for many veterans, the anguish of returning addicted is added to the usual burdens of readjusting to civilian life. Moreover, there are no welcoming parades awaiting the men who fought a war that stands as a monument to deception and greed, a departure from our democratic traditions revived in World War II, an incredible inhumanity in the conduct of the war and in administration unconcern for solutions to major social problems at home.

That a revitalization of American ethics and values is long overdue was made clear by Fred J. Cook's exposé, "The Corrupt Society" (*The Nation,* June 1–8, 1963), in which he described the impact of the "ethics" of corporate executives on Americans—not merely adults but adolescents as well; the latter in cheating on examinations, in the purchase of master's and doctoral theses, and so on. This influence is epitomized in public reaction to the incident in which a 50-year-old Negro janitor had returned $240,000 he had found to Brink's, the armored car service. Had he not, he would never be able to "look my three kids in the face again." After returning the money he found himself the subject of ridicule and harassment; his sons taunted by their classmates that their father "was dumb, a fool and stupid." In the conclusion of this episode, "Unexpected Rewards of Virtue," Cook notes:

> In a monied society, Douglas Johnson had committed the cardinal sin; acting on an honest impulse, he had returned a fortune that he might have kept. In the contrast between his harrowing experience and the virtual indifference that greeted the tale of two bribe-takers in the Billy Sol Estes case, for instance, one finds a barometer that accurately gauges the shabbiness of our ethical standards.

America's prevailing ethic, one that runs through the entire forty-four pages of Cook's exposé is, obviously, "Don't get caught."

Lest the reader believe that there has been a decrease in corporate "crime" against the American people, the recently published book by Mintz and Cohen[103] brings the status of corporate corruption and largely unpublicized "crime" up-to-date in Chapter 8, "Crime in the Suites." A recent report of Ralph Nader's study group, entitled "The Closed Enterprise System," charged that the American public in the past twenty years have been cheated of "billions of dollars annually in higher prices, lost production, excessive pollution and lack of innovation because of the practice of monopolies," which are being protected from antitrust actions through the intervention "by members of Congress and of the White House staff, as well as by the lack of enthusiasm for antitrust matters of some of the very people in the Justice Department responsible for them."[103]

Contrast this protection of corporations and the protection of profits by their exclusion from the wage-price freeze, in which it is wages alone that are effectively controlled, with the lack of concern for the health and welfare of our returning veterans for whom even adequate medical care is in short supply. Jim Castelli, assistant editor of the *Catholic News* in New York, reports in *The Nation* of September 6, 1971, that "One of the most incomprehensible tragedies of the Indochinese war has been the shabby treatment of the men who have had to fight . . . When they return they can't find work—almost 400,000 of them are unemployed; they may have become addicted to heroin while in Southeast Asia [and available treatment facilities are largely ineffective, especially in the face of rising unemployment]; and conditions in most Veterans Administration hospitals make proper treatment and rehabilitation virtually impossible."

Although hearings conducted by Senator Alan Cranston (D., Calif.) for the Veterans Affairs Subcommittee in November and December 1969 unearthed many of these problems and a *"Life* article helped push through a $105 million budget increase, this is still less than the amount the subcommittee recommended." Unfortunately, it was learned at subsequent hearings in April 1971, that the entire $105,-000,000 had been spent without "a penny used to hire new medical staff, the system's most urgent need; and there has been a cutback in the average daily census . . . ," this despite the fact that there are now "5,000 veterans on waiting lists . . ." Although some additional staff have been hired, "staff shortages are responsible for a complete breakdown in post-operative care and rehabilitation." The author explains this lack of concern: "But no matter the will of Congress, it seems that the final say will belong to the budget office and the Veterans Administration, both of which are far more committed to 'holding down inflation' and saving money than to providing adequate health care for veterans." Castelli also states that:

> The most macabre aspect of the whole VA Hospital question is the existence of what Cranston calls "a new kind of body count"—it is a body count of the lives of American soldiers lost because of failure to provide them with proper medical support . . .

The author concludes:

> We have cheated in this area of our national life long enough. Either we are going to gear up and provide the bed space and staff necessary to take care of our veterans or else we will incur for the rest of this century the bitterness and wrath of those who have fought for us.

If, as the psychiatrist, Dr. Brian Joseph, interviewed in the ABC-TV program, "Heroes and Heroin," stated, conditions in Vietnam resembling those in American ghettos were partly responsible for susceptibility to using heroin, then certainly failure to improve those economic and social conditions for returning veterans may reduce motivation for seeking treatment on the part of the addicted veterans.

Some idea of the contributing causes to an increase in the spread of heroin use is apparent from a sensitive report in *The Nation* of September 20, 1971, entitled "Back From Vietnam: The Sense of Isolation," in which the author, Murray Polner, describes the adjustment of veterans who have been home for about three years. Polner had interviewed 204 Vietnam veterans for a book he was writing while teaching in a community college outside of New York City. He is currently executive assistant to the Chancellor of the New York City Public Schools, and the author of *No Victory Parades: The Return of the Vietnam Veteran* (Holt, Rinehart & Winston); and of a forthcoming book, *When Can I Come Home: A Debate on Amnesty,* to be published by Doubleday in an Anchor edition.

Polner notes the difference between those who returned in 1969 when jobs were more available and those who returned in the subsequent period, and describes the reluctance of black veterans to enroll in opportunities for education—partly because of lack of preparation and partly out of fear of discrimination and distrust of the Establishment. Of special relevance is his summary that "among the few researchers who have started to think seriously about the men home from Vietnam there is nearly unanimous agreement that despite the many who seem to be adjusting easily, a surprisingly large number are not," adding that "unsettling reports" have begun to pour into the Washington VA headquarters in response to a letter from the Chief Medical Director to VA personnel throughout the nation, asking for their descriptions of the new veterans. The reports can be briefly summarized: A substantial number are returning "embittered, distrustful, emotionally disturbed, even brutalized by their experience."

The amnesty program, "announced with much fanfare and great expectations, has never really gotten off the ground," according to a report in *The Nation* by Samuel A. Simon, now serving as a captain in the Judge Advocate General's Corps, U.S. Army. (The author makes clear that the article represents his own views and does not reflect those of the Department of the Army or the Department of Defense.) "Of the veterans who had returned, one said, 'you are told it won't be on your record; but then they send in all sorts of reports and soon' everybody on earth knows he's a drug addict and they just start taking more drugs." It was also noted that many commanders are not sympathetic to the amnesty program.

Simon provides additional details regarding the "catch" in the program, namely, that despite assurances from "everyone from the soldier's company commander to the President of the United States, that if he turns himself in as a drug user, no punitive action will be taken . . . more and more soldiers are finding that in actuality amnesty doesn't mean amnesty . . . It applies only to the crime of possession and use of drugs. It does not apply to possession of large amounts of drugs, to selling drugs, or to drug-related offenses. Thus the heroin addict returning from Vietnam finds that he must steal to support his habit in the United States, and that when he turns himself in he will be subject to court-martial for theft . . ." Also, only after a soldier enters the drug amnesty program, according to Simon, does he learn that this *automatically* cuts off all veteran and disability benefits for treatment of drug-related injury or disease to which he might otherwise be entitled after leaving the service. Moreover, he is also required to add to the length of his tour of duty the time spent in treatment.

He finds in addition "that a number of other adverse consequences threaten him when he submits to treatment under drug amnesty, among them loss of security clearance and job transfers." Although "many soldiers would no doubt want to enter the program even with full knowledge of all the dangers, the problem is that the average soldier is rarely fully informed and relies instead on false assurances from the President and members of the military establishment . . . The result is that most soldiers do not become aware of the hazards of participating until they have gone beyond the point of no return, i.e., he must accept all the losses—benefits, extension of tour of duty, loss of security clearance, etc. or withdraw from amnesty and be prosecuted on the drug use offense," and hence the title "The Catch in Amnesty."

In view of our own dramatic failure to arrest the epidemic of heroin addiction, and the added problems of the GI heroin addicts, it is difficult to understand why, until recently, a veritable "blackout" on the British plan of controlling heroin has prevailed. Every heroin addict in England, far from being considered a criminal, is eligible for the medical treatment considered appropriate and possible for him. Rehabilitation begins with the first contact following registration. This may range from gradual withdrawal, to methadone maintenance or heroin maintenance, with a whole range of rehabilitative services available to him. There is no need for the addict to steal to support his habit; as a result, there is no crime associated with addiction. Here it is estimated that the need of the addict to pay for an expensive habit accounts for 50 to 80 percent of the crime in New

York City. There is no need for the addict to push heroin onto others to earn money for his own habit; as a result, the infection ceases.

It is not surprising, therefore, that, as reported in *The Manchester Guardian* of August 6, 1971, by the end of 1970 there was an actual decrease in the number of registered heroin addicts. A report of the British Advisory Committee on Drug Dependence to the Home Office also indicated a considerable decrease in the amount of heroin being prescribed since 1968, and a slight increase in the amount of methadone. We can only *guess* at the number of addicts in the United States but by all indications it is increasing at an alarming rate. (See Appendix E.)

It is therefore welcome news that "powerful and respectable interests" in America "have finally concluded that the vast irrationality and hypocrisy of the country's attitude toward drugs are deeply destructive and should be turned around," according to *The Village Voice* of July 15, 1971. The reporter, Kenneth Brodney, cites a recommendation of a report that was undertaken for the Ford Foundation, a report that has been distributed among all members of the Mayor's Narcotics Control Council in New York City and sent to "hundreds of other influential policy makers throughout the country." The recommendation suggests "eliminating criminal penalties for possession for personal use," because this approach has created widespread disrespect for the drug laws and has possibly done more to encourage than to discourage illegal drug use, undercutting bona fide prevention and education.

"The report hammers away at the essential failure of the nation's efforts and leadership in virtually every area of the problem: in education programs, in basic research to fill in the enormous gaps in knowledge of how drugs really act on the body and brain, and in the treatment of most drug abusers." As to what ought to be done, Brodney cites from the report:

"There is one method of treatment that has not been attempted in this country since the Bureau of Narcotics (now the Bureau of Narcotics and Dangerous Drugs of the Department of Justice), with the support of the American Medical Association, stamped it out in the early 1920's. The Bureau succeeded in banning [some 40 heroin maintenance clinics throughout the country] by 1923, and has since done everything possible to discredit this method of treatment." The authors of the method "do not propose the immediate, widespread adoption of heroin maintenance in the United States . . . but they note that, according to Ford's own careful study of the variation of this method used in Britain, it 'appears to have succeeded in containing the narcotic problem in that country at this time.' "

It is apparent from the evidence presented thus far that the persistence of a highly unrealistic and ineffective method of controlling heroin addiction for four decades, in the face of evidence that another method during the same period has proved effective, suggests either a deeply rooted prejudice toward heroin addicts, a majority of whom (about 75 percent) are black and Puerto Rican, or is indicative of a callous lack of concern about providing solutions to drug abuse and addiction. That is as true of the GI problems of heroin addiction as it is of the addiction problems at home.

It is thus particularly disturbing to read former Attorney General John N. Mitchell's statement at a police dinner in Atlanta that "the dope pushers have moved into Britain in a big way and are providing narcotics to the addict over and above what he received through medical care." In contrast, Mitchell said the Administration in America "was making significant progress against drug abuse by giving priority to stopping the drug traffic." *The Manchester Guardian* of May 19, 1971, from which the above is taken ("US attacks British Drug Surrender"), states:

> British authorities have no evidence of any large-scale operators in the injectable drugs field—heroin, cocaine and methadone. Lady Wootton, a former member of the Committee on Drug Dependence, said last night that the charges were "totally untrue." She added: "He does not know what he is talking about. People who live in glass houses should not throw stones."

The report notes that "the basic British approach to the narcotics problem is to encourage drug addicts to seek treatment. If they do, they have no assurance that they will continue to be prescribed supplies of drugs, but they do know that they will be treated as patients and not dealt with under prison, or prison-like conditions, as often happens in the USA."

It is apparent that the public needs to be informed of the failure of our government to be concerned, noting particularly the lack of treatment facilities in ghetto neighborhoods. Lindesmith, a noted authority on narcotic addiction, recommends that the first step in reform might well be a conference sponsored by the American Medical Association with the New York Academy of Medicine at the invitation of the Secretary of the Treasury and the Attorney General, "with a mandate to revise the existing regulations so as to bring them into conformity with the Supreme Court's doctrine that addiction is a proper subject of medical care." Lindesmith also suggests that delegates to such a conference should be predominantly medical practitioners with direct clinical experience with addicts, especially in private practice. Threat of criminal prosecution against physicians who undertake care for addicts should be eliminated through revision of Treasury Department regulations. This, Lindesmith believes, might make it feasible for the medical conference to bring to full public examination "the facts concerning addicts who are now being handled as medical cases and shielded from the police and punitive action."

He makes clear that there are "presently privileged addicts to whom the usual penalties and rules are not applied, who are given access to drugs legally and handled medically." He also indicates that there does not seem to be "a single instance of a country in which opiate addiction is handled medically where the use of opiates has acquired the status of a fad or become an epidemic as it has in the United States . . ." Lindesmith adds that the use of addicting drugs by young persons is a matter of especially serious concern. "The evidence seems to indicate quite clearly that the situation most favorable for the spread of drug use among young persons is the one in which addiction is dealt with as a criminal matter and one which includes a flourishing illicit traffic. It is in this situation that drugs become glamorous and attractive to youth, and these are also the conditions which seem to favor the creation of subcultures of drug users which, by recruitment of new members, tend to become self-perpetuating."[104]

## Long-Term Advantages of a Medical Program

One of the gaps in our knowledge of addiction is the lack of reliable information about our addicts. It hardly needs to be said that a medical program automatically generates more reliable statistical and other data than does a police program. According to Lindesmith, in most European countries figures available from druggists and doctors tell most of the story of addiction, and police data contribute only a minor supplement. He also refers to a study made by Dr. John O'Donnell in Kentucky of former patients at the Public Health Service Hospital at Lexington, who observed that "many of those who were abstaining from drugs had moved away from the sources of illicit drugs into communities where there was no illicit market or where they did not 'know the ropes.' " O'Donnell concludes that "this factor of unavailability may go far in explaining the high rate of abstinence in this group [relatively rural], in contrast to previous follow-up studies which were conducted in, or included large metropolitan areas where the illegal narcotics market has never been completely abolished."[105]

Aside from the fact that gaps in our knowledge will be filled under a medical program, it will be possible to demonstrate how the availability acts as a stimulant when addicts have been temporarily or even more permanently rehabilitated. Among the adolescents I have interviewed who have been able to throw off heroin addiction with little more than strong support from an adult or older friend, neither of whom used drugs, the stimulus was extreme difficulty in obtaining heroin in a new setting, in several instances when the adolescents went off to college.

Not only do we not lessen and remove the availability of drugs, but we compound the problem by the injustice in the disproportion between the punishment meted out to the trafficker and that reserved for the drug user. In short, the message that is conveyed to our youth is that our Establishment is not *really* interested in stopping the availability of drugs. This implication is confirmed not merely by the failure to seek out those responsible for the source of illegal drugs, but also by the unleashing of a nearly pure heroin in South Vietnam and Indochina where our government, through the Pentagon, is in control and the illegal traffic could not take place without our knowledge. The availability to the GI's could not occur without our support, as the ABC-News TV documentary has already shown.

Dr. Joel Fort in his book, *The Pleasure Seekers,* refers to studies sponsored by the United Nations and the World Health Organization as well as his own investigations, confirming cultivation of opium in the Golden Triangle, described in the opening part of the ABC-TV News program processed into heroin in Thailand and Hongkong, and then, as the ABC news reporter indicated, made available to our GI's in Vietnam.

Fort also makes clear that "this large and successful traffic requires extensive collusion with Thai officials and considerable corruption, including bribery and profiteering by officials, high and low, in the government including the police and the army. All of this despite the continued presence of two American agents of the Federal Bureau of Narcotics in Bangkok whose obligation under the law is to expose and cut off the traffic in narcotics." To this Fort adds that along the more dangerous part of the journey between the Golden Triangle and Bangkok "for internal use and *for distribution to the rest of Asia and to the United States,* the opium products are guarded by Chinese Nationalist troops who settled in the area following Chiang Kai-shek's expulsion from the mainland . . ." subsequently maintaining themselves with "illicit narcotics profits and, according to some reports, with additional subsidies from the American Central Intelligence Agency *as a 'bulwark against Communism.'* " [Italics added.] Fort concludes:

> In effect, the United States is covering up and sometimes subsidizing the opium traffic which it purports to be eradicating.

Much more recently, according to an article in the May 1971 issue of *Ramparts,* by Frank Browning and Banning Garrett, entitled "The

New Opium War," the major source of illegal opium today is in Southeast Asia, where the growers, processors, and distributors are protected by our allies—the governments of Laos, Thailand, and South Vietnam . . . The authors further state that our misguided policies "play a major role in a process that has already rerouted the opium traffic from the Middle East to Southeast Asia and is every day opening new channels for its shipment to the U.S." (See also Appendix D.)

Additional confirmation of the situation with respect to the heroin traffic in Southeast Asia is provided by a series of ten articles in *The Christian Science Monitor,* three of which are discussed below. The first of the series, is headed "We're dealing with an epidemic" (May 29, 1970).

In his travels on the trail of drugs, John Hughes, now the editor, found that "in Laos some of the main growers of illegal opium are tough mountain tribesmen upon whom the American Central Intelligence Agency (CIA) relies heavily in the campaign against the Communists. Opium is the principal cash crop in the non-Communist part of the country. Clearly, the CIA is cognizant of, if not party to the extensive movement of opium out of Laos.

"One charter pilot told me that 'friendly' opium shipments get special CIA clearance and monitoring on their flights southward out of the country. The same source alleged two or three flights without this 'protection' crashed under mysterious circumstances.

"A five-month investigation by this newspaper into the international narcotics traffic reveals that illicit drugs are swirling like a floodtide down the clandestine channels that lead to the addict user.

"To the United States, the principal consuming country, the flow is massive, and increasing. True, seizures are up. Heroin seizures by American customs agents have increased 1,200 percent over the past five years. The Nixon administration is devoting major effort to disrupting the traffic. At home and abroad American narcotics agents are doing a yeoman job. Whether shooting it out with opium traffickers in Turkey, or penetrating the heroin factories of Marseille, France, they are often men of remarkable courage, working undercover for long periods at considerable risk. But the market for narcotics has expanded phenomenally, too. Some believe it has doubled in the past six months. It now caters to 11- and 12-year-olds. President Nixon says 180,000 Americans are addicted to heroin. Each requires several 'fixes' a day of the white powder that has brought death to hundreds and so-called 'living death' to thousands more." Nixon's estimate is low even for New York City, in the author's view.

Ironically, increased governmental attention to the drug traffic has boosted the current flow. Traffickers fear that traditional sources and

channels may be sealed off. So they have been moving large consignments while they can." Hughes notes that "even if production
could be wiped out overnight, enough has been stockpiled to meet
world demand for several years. The United Nations says the drug
traffic is snowballing and that it is 'imperatively urgent' to find ways
to cope with it. A top American narcotics agent puts it more bluntly,
'We're dealing with an epidemic.' "

Hughes reports that with no special entree to underworld circles,
"it was possible, with time and money, to buy every major illegal
drug. In Afghanistan, Pakistan, and Thailand, I came easily to the
point of purchase for opium. *In Laos I could have bought it by the
small planeload.*" [Italics added.] He notes that such purchases could
be duplicated in India, Turkey, or Mexico. "In Hong Kong I need
walk but a few steps from my office to get the distinctive scent of
smoking opium from the neighborhood vendor. In Beirut a Western
diplomat offered me introductions to cocaine sellers in a number of
night clubs . . . But in Marseille I could have bought top-grade
heroin by the kilo (2.2 pounds). It would have taken an advance
payment of $3,000 and several days' isolation in a hotel room while
the sellers checked me out. . . . So skillful and careful are the
traffickers, however, that the transaction would have been completed
without my ever meeting the deliverer . . . As for hashish and marijuana, I could have bought this as easily as toothpaste or candy
throughout much of Asia, the Middle East, and parts of Mexico. In
Afghanistan, hashish sellers distribute pamphlets advertising their
own special brands."

An alarming aspect of this traffic is Hughes's description of the
distribution and availability of synthetic drugs—"the amphetamines,
the barbiturates, the hallucinogens—the trail started no farther than
the beach in front of my home in Hong Kong. There the pushers are
trying to proposition American children from the international school
nearby. American schools in Bangkok, Thailand, and Ankara, Turkey, have encountered similar problems." The reporter describes in
some detail the hazards of smuggling across international borders for
foreigners, especially Americans, with "several hundred Americans
having had tormented personal experience of this. They are serving
long sentences for narcotics offenses in such hellholes as Sands prison,
just outside Beirut. . . . Despite the hazards, the profits from drug
smuggling are immense. If transported successfully to the U.S. and cut
into 45,000 packets for individual users, a kilo of heroin that costs a
few thousand dollars in Marseille sells for more than a quarter of a
million dollars. With this kind of money to be made, involvement in
the narcotics traffic extends into the most pseudo-respectable circles
and into the highest ranks of a number of governments."

Hughes adds to this tale of horror: "In one Asian country, an American diplomat told me: 'We want the drug traffic out of here stopped. But we have a problem. If American narcotics agents start nosing around here too closely, they're going to uncover some links to pretty high places.' In Laos the Army is involved in the opium business, and Lao Air Force planes transport opium. In Thailand the massive outflow of narcotics could hardly take place without collaboration at fairly high levels. In the past, involvement in the drug traffic has extended into the Cabinet. It may still today."

In a subsequent article (June 16, 1970), Hughes wrote, "For the junk merchants of Southeast Asia, Thailand is the corridor through which their illegal merchandise must pass to Hong Kong and the lucrative markets of America." Burma is a top producer, but the Laotians "are deeply engaged in opium business . . . Dominating the protection business are the Chinese Nationalist soldiers left over from the war with the Communists . . . The Lao Army is deep in the money-spinning opium business, and Lao Air Force planes transport opium. Some private pilots say the Air Force's opium runs are made with CIA 'protection.' " To this Hughes adds: "In these countries narcotic trafficking involves people in high places." He reports:

> During this year's Communist offensive, the military cut back on its opium activities. The main reason was not, according to one well-placed source, because they were preoccupied with the Communists. It was concern lest a wave of newspaper correspondents, in town for the crisis, got wind of the opium operations.

"In Peking," Hughes continues, "the Communist regime has imposed stiff penalties for drug usage and illegal production. But that Peking can effectively police the opium growers in Yunnan seems doubtful. There must also be substantial authorized production for the medicinal needs of more than 700 million Chinese. This affords the opportunity for diversion to illegal use. Thus China undoubtedly makes its contribution to the illegal narcotics traffic.

"But there is no evidence of a massive and calculated campaign by Peking to flood non-Communist countries with debilitating narcotics. Some Westerners have charged the Chinese with just such a plan. But interviews with hundreds of narcotics experts in the past 5 months have failed to produce the proof."

Says one non-American expert: "With their U-2's, their satellites, the Americans would soon have evidence of any large-scale opium production in China. Presumably, they would be happy to make it public. Certainly, drugs come out of China but there's no proof that the Peking regime is organizing it all."

The "opium comes down the trails through Burma and Laos. Some bypasses Thailand. It is flown out of Laos by pilots of fortune of various nationalities operating a fictitious airline called 'Air Opium.' Some cargoes are dropped in watertight bags in the Gulf of Siam and picked up by rendezvousing ships. Others are flown into Vietnam . . . White heroin is smuggled to the United States by couriers on commercial and military flights. Purple heroin, morphine and opium destined for such local markets as Hong Kong travels by sea. See Appendix E.

"In Bangkok's twin city of Thonburi is hidden a clandestine laboratory which converts morphine to heroin. Local addicts buy red or purple, or No. 3 heroin, about 60 to 70 percent pure. White, or No. 4 heroin is purer and of export grade. This is destined for the American market."

Hughes raises the question: "How to reduce the traffic?", reporting "a United Nations survey recommends upgrading the living standards of the hill tribes and substituting cash crops like peas, tobacco, tea and coffee for opium, but this is a long-term program and would cost millions. With present uncertainties in Indo-China great areas of opium-growing countries would remain unreachable. For the moment, eradication seems unattainable. Hope must be placed on seizures by Asian narcotics officers and on American narcotics agents assigned to such cities as Bangkok, Singapore, Saigon and Hong Kong to gather and coordinate intelligence on traffickers. The other part of the solution lies in the education and reform of drug users themselves. But that is another story."

In his June 19 story, Hughes notes that Hong Kong "has been nurtured on the opium trade and is still today a focal point for the flow of narcotics throughout the Far East. Its own addicts (80,000 in a population of 4 million) give Hong Kong one of the highest narcotics addiction rates in the world . . . Drugs are also transshipped through Hong Kong to other destinations in Asia and to the profitable markets of the United States and the Canadian West Coast."

## Round-the-Clock Smuggling

In a supplementary dispatch from Saigon under date of June 16, 1970, Hughes began his report, headlined "GIs, Narcotics and Vietnam": "The Vietnam war has opened up dozens of new channels to the men who move narcotics illegally around the world."

The "thousands of military aircraft" and "hundreds of ships" that provide support for the American military and fly on a round-the-clock schedule to and from Saigon's Tan San Ut Airport ("one of the busiest in the world") ". . . offer broad opportunity for narcotics smuggling . . . The bigger planes fly routinely between Vietnam and the United States. Others shuttle back and forth between bases in Japan, Taiwan, Thailand, and the Philippines. Customs inspection between countries is often cursory. Sometimes it is omitted."

Heroin destined for the American market is smuggled regularly by servicemen who "are the prey of professional narcotics rings or in business for themselves." Opportunities for this clandestine traffic include the five-day rest-and-recuperation leaves every six months, with the resultant "movement between Vietnamese airport and R&R centers like Hong Kong, Manila, Taipei"; mail sent home by servicemen, who, according to Myles J. Ambrose, Commissioner of United States Customs, "are using their APO privileges to ship an 'increasing quantity' of dangerous drugs" in gifts purchased by servicemen at discount prices at the China Fleet Club in Hong Kong and shipped home through the military post office.

Although narcotics agents concentrate on professional smugglers of hard drugs, a "very serious" problem also exists in the use and movement of marijuana by American servicemen in Vietnam.

Among steps taken to stem the traffic in opiates was a general court-martial and sentencing of a U.S. Air Force pilot to sixteen years at hard labor for smuggling opium. Australian authorities have warned of curtailments of the R&R program in their country, and police in Hong Kong are worried. Military authorities in Vietnam have moved to reduce production (estimated at 100,000 kilos a year), American narcotics agents are training South Vietnam agents, "major educational programs are under way among the troops, and marijuana crops are destroyed when detected." [The ABC news TV program discussed earlier in this chapter does not suggest the possibility that South Vietnam would be interested in eradicating heroin.]

"But the task is major. Meanwhile the narcotics traffickers take advantage of opportunities afforded them by the confusion and disruption of war."[106]

Clearly the flow of drugs to the United States is not likely to be stopped until the war ends and we get out of Southeast Asia. It is also clear that the stockpiling in the United States, of heroin in particular, to which *The Christian Science Monitor* staff writer refers, means that unless alternative solutions are sought we are likely to be plagued with serious problems of drug abuse and addiction for a very long time. Given the status of the problem on an international scale, only a solution that takes the profit out of drug traffic will be effective in stopping what appears to be an international epidemic, the worst being in the United States.

On the other hand, the evidence provided in this chapter suggests that at the very least we have a major responsibility to stop the traffic where we have been in control for so many years. See Appendix E.

The United Nations reports to which presumably Dr. Fort refers (earlier in the chapter) confirm major sources of illicit opium production in the Yunnan-Burma-Laos-Thailand region where "it has been estimated that the annual production of opium amounted to 1,000 tons . . ." as of 1966. Since much more money is made out of transforming the raw opium into morphine and heroin, and transportation of opium is difficult because of its bulk, weight, smell, etc., the report indicates that "the traffickers now try to extract the morphine near the source of production." The Commission noted that the illicit traffic "was a well-established and profitable business extending all over the world. The traffic was mainly supported by supplies diverted at the stage of the production of the raw materials . . . The bulk of the raw drugs, however, came from large expanses of cultivation carried out illegally, and in areas that were often remote; this applied to opium produced illegally or without adequate supervision in Southeast Asia, and in certain countries of the Middle East."[107]

It was also noted that "Opium and the opiates continued to be a serious problem in the Far East. A new development was the smuggling into Hong Kong of large consignments of opium and morphine concealed in ordinary cargoes."

The following news dispatch from Henry Kamm to *The New York Times* from Vientiane, Laos (October 27, 1969) provides evidence of concern by a Senate subcommittee, meeting "in closed session" to investigate the obscure war that has been raging for years in the kingdom of Laos. The article is the second in a series by correspondents of *The New York Times* giving the background of what has been called the " 'twilight war' in the remote interior of Laos." In that article, Kamm describes Gen. Vang Pao as a leader of Laotian forces of Meo hill people, estimated at 40,000, against Communist-led forces. There is reason to believe the opium traffic in this area, which involves the Meo tribesmen, is in some way connected with the "twilight war." Kamm adds: "Although American officials are not permitted to discuss the subject, their occasional lapses leave little doubt that the general's backing comes from the United States Central Intelligence Agency. This impression was sustained during three weeks of discussions with the best-informed Laotian and American officials here." Kamm notes that "The general travels to Thailand often. It is believed that he confers there with CIA officials, but American officials say he goes to see his doctor. On his first visit to the United States, he went to Fort Bragg in North Carolina, where the Special Forces train."

A *New York Times* editorial of June 10, 1970, "Subversion by CIA," states: "The disclosure that the American economic aid mission in Laos is being used as a cover for intelligence operations in Laos is nothing less than a body blow to the credibility of the peaceful presence of the United States in neutral and friendly nations. The decision to allow the Central Intelligence Agency to subvert an important foreign mission was made during the Kennedy Administration in 1962. The fact that it has thus persisted under three Presidents dramatizes the extent to which the debasement of national and diplomatic ethics has become a nonpartisan evil . . ." The editorial concludes: "Unless these questions are frankly answered, the nation's friends abroad and its youth at home will become increasingly cynical about all American claims and goals. It is the road to alienation and isolationism. This is a price this country cannot afford to pay." See Appendix E.

A 1971 UN Bulletin on Narcotics reports "considerable local uncontrolled production of opium" in Thailand that is of world concern because "it also attracts additional supplies from Burma and Laos." Much of this opium "is converted into morphine and heroin, mainly for local consumption, though some flows into international illicit channels."

Subsequent UN reports from Thailand "indicate that the situation [as reported in 1966] has not materially improved since that time. On the contrary, it would seem that the problem has been exacerbated by increased resort to opium alkaloids and their derivatives in addition to opium." The reports also indicate that "clandestine heroin laboratories have been discovered, and in 1967 the seizures of illicit heroin rose sharply to 226 kilograms . . . five times the previous average. Even more startling was the seizure in 1968 of 474 kilograms of morphine, another 400 percent increase. At the same time, opium seizures remained at a very high level."

The circumstances "surrounding opium production in Laos were reported to be similar to those in Thailand." The Permanent Central Board stated it had no information to show that the situation had in any way improved since a 1966 report, adding "On the other hand, remedial measures would scarcely be feasible in the disturbed conditions now prevailing in that region."[108]

Concern over Thailand's role in the illicit traffic in opium and heroin has caused Representative Lester Wolff, of New York, a member of the House Foreign Affairs Committee who recently returned from a fact-finding study mission, to urge curtailment of funds to that country which are currently slated to be increased from $28.5 million to $35 million.

The continuing anxiety of the International Narcotics Control Board over the situation in Thailand is somewhat mitigated by the knowledge that this is shared by the government of Thailand, which has asked the assistance of the United States in "devising and applying remedial measures," by diversifying the agricultural economy and re-

placing poppy cultivation with substitute crops that would yield a cash
income. However, until these goals are achieved, there is concern on
two counts: that traditional consumption of opium in Thailand has
given way to heroin addiction; and because of "the ever-present danger" of the country's becoming a major center of international illicit
traffic. "Already there are signs that the Board's apprehensions in this
latter respect are well-grounded and that international illicit traffickers
are turning their attention to Southeast Asia as their accustomed
sources of supply in the Mediterranean and in the Near East begin
to be narrowed."[109]

The above confirms what *The Christian Science Monitor* articles
have indicated. The question that disturbs me is why our forces are
so powerless to control the illicit traffic where we are in authority if
our government is genuinely interested in stopping the source of the
heroin traffic. Certainly what is happening to the addicted GI's makes
the answer to my question even more urgent.

On the basis of the foregoing evidence of duplicity and official
evasion of our own laws regarding traffic in illegal heroin, the
reluctance of the Bureau of Narcotics and Dangerous Drugs to consider any alternative plan to control heroin addiction becomes even
more illogical. If there were not already a credibility gap, one would
certainly result. It has to be assumed that the Department of Justice
has been aware that the source of illegal heroin is now in the very
countries that are under our control. If even there we are unwilling
to take the necessary steps to prevent the flow of heroin, how can
we justify a policy that continues to punish only the user?

Looked at realistically, our present punitive approach to the control of drugs utilizes the logic of the Judge in Samuel Butler's
*Erewhon* who, before passing sentence on a man who had been ac-
cused many times before of "pulmonary consumption," comments:
"You say that it is your misfortune to be criminal: I answer that it is
your crime to be unfortunate." In the case of our youth involved with
drugs, their "crime" is to be young and immature enough to be influenced by the availability of illegal heroin and other drugs; unfortunate enough not to be needed by our society, except as passive consumers, whose potential contributions to the creative reform of our
society are unused and unwanted; and unfortunate enough to belong
to groups in our society whose basic needs, material and nonmaterial,
continue to be ignored and neglected.

Adult society can no longer justify and defend punishment for the
user of drugs when the real "villain" is a society in which the economy,
by virtue of a single-minded goal of financial profit and the power
that accrues to wealth in our society, refuses even to envision the possibility of employment for all, far beyond the number currently un-

employed. Unrestrained by competition and profiting from subsidies and allowances, powerful corporations "have turned our country into a welfare state" for their benefit. Moreover, they do not consider it any part of their responsibility to provide employment in rebuilding our cities if only in partial repayment for the stealing of public wealth that makes what heroin addicts take from the public in order to support their habit seem insignificant. It would be only simple justice in view of the enormous benefits (in little or no taxation, to cite one example) they have received and continue to receive from the government.[110]

In the public sector of the nation, there is an unlimited need for employment, in our rural areas despoiled by greed, as well as in our ghettos, where urban renewal has been described in *Fortune* as the removal of the Negro. Such a vision of full employment could transform the New York subway system, for example, from a filthy wasteland, where human beings are thrown into close but meaningless contact, into an attractive means of public transportation that would make the inhabitants of even such cities as New York feel they are a part of the human race.

Instead of continuing the pattern of destroying historic landmarks to make way for roads, the planners of which look upon cities as places you drive through as fast as possible; or instead of destroying genuine communities in which the remaining residents, largely black, Puerto Rican, and poor white families, had genuine roots, to make way for office buildings, the remaining communities could be rebuilt as a way of demonstrating that cities can become livable places, with surroundings that restore some of the natural environment that was the city's before the age of the "robber barons," as they were called in an earlier period.

Foolish? I can hear some of you . . . Too late, you think? Not if we do more than just dream and imagine those transformations while under the influence of "mind-altering" or "mind-expanding" drugs. If those drugs do, indeed, have the latter effect, how does it happen that so few are disturbed by the ravages of the giant corporations— ravages not unique to the cities, just more noticeable and obviously on a much larger scale. More important, if the psychoactive drugs in widespread use today stimulate and expand consciousness, how does it happen that so few see the waste as a challenge to rebuild? How does it happen that so many of you—who know what I am saying and have rejected work in the corporations whose enticements until recently have lured so many college graduates into the corporate world —are abandoning your own roots for a kind of privatism that may be a natural sequel to drug use but is again, as I indicated in Chapter II, doing precisely what the Establishment is doing all in its power to achieve—to relieve government of any responsibility to underwrite the rebuilding of America.

Rather, could not youth ally itself with adults in a common effort to challenge the government to meet our long neglected needs and to create a truly human society? That is the dream youth should be having if drugs really enriched our vision of a good life. Or is the effect like that of much of television; it is stimulating and exciting but does not leave one with any responsibility for action since the watching and listening are almost entirely passive. Some of the young generation have been able, once free of the need to be involved with drugs, to think aloud with me about the meaning of drug taking, which many describe as an escape from the reality that confronts youth. As one young person put it: "If young people are alienating themselves from society, it simply means that they are dissatisfied, and do not know how to handle their feelings in a constructive manner. Drug use, in this respect, serves both as an escape and a symptom of rebellion." This person recognizes the problems the country is facing and the potential of youth for solving them. *"But* if this potential is to be realized, it must be guided, perhaps even prodded, by responsible, concerned, and knowledgeable adults."

As evidence of need for guidance, many of the young who are using drugs point to the basis for "teenage disrespect of the educational system and of teachers." Some have said: "The plain fact is that students want more of an education than they have been receiving. Many teachers are not sufficiently equipped to handle the student's ever-growing needs." And I would agree. It is unfortunate that for students to have ready access not merely to the usual guidance personnel but to any teacher with whom they feel comfortable, they have to define their problem as a psychological one, so conditioned are adults to viewing human problems as adjustment, to rather than them as arising out of interaction with environment. Many young drug abusers have told me that one reason for becoming part of the drug cult is to find some basis for identification, to achieve a sense of "belonging."

However, those individuals have added that this involves relinquishing to some extent control over one's life, as there are "rules to obey, rules that soon begin to exert their own kind of pressure." To that I would like to add from my own observations that the pressures just referred to have sometimes dehumanized the drug users. I am referring to the panic that occurs when one of the group has a bad trip and the reactions to this are vastly different from the caring kind of reactions that today's youths claim to have for one another. I have known personally of instances in which deaths have occurred in a drug-taking group when the other members were unwilling to provide hospital authorities information about the drugs out of fear of becoming involved. Another instance occurred during a Christmas campus party when a young girl, confused by drugs and alcohol, left the group and no one was concerned enough to follow her outside. The next morning her frozen body was discovered on the campus. Is it possible that one of the effects of today's psychoactive drugs is to lessen the sense of mutual concern and responsibility, and that the feeling of togetherness attributed to drugs is a spurious one?

The changed behavior that some of the young people have described becomes apparent at the time the drug user is becoming concerned enough over the effects to want "out." As one thoughtful young girl put it: "Choosing to leave the drug scene or to become more deeply involved in it is a hard and sometimes frightening decision. The person who desires to break the hold of drugs must believe in his own ability to do so. He must expect setbacks and be determined not to be discouraged by them."

Especially important is what she adds: "He must decide that there is a place in society for him, and that if he hopes to achieve any personal fulfillment at all, he must set goals for himself and then, slowly, try to reach these goals. The decision to leave the drug culture is more a commitment than a decision. At this point, though, outside help should be made available." And much of this help has to come from the adult world which should see the former drug user, as so many adolescents have put it, as a "victim" of a "drugged society."

CHAPTER IX

# *The Alternatives . . .*

And such is the irresistible nature of truth that all it asks, and all
it wants, is the liberty of appearing.

—THOMAS PAINE

It is not accidental that full-time and committed political activists
are rarely intensive drug users; it is also important that the full-
time denizens of the drug-using hippie subculture are rarely capable of sustained political activity. Sustained engagement in an
effort to change the world is rarely compatible with the kind of
self-absorption and inwardness that results from intensive and
regular drug use; however strongly the committed drug user may
feel about the inequities of American society, his primary efforts
are usually directed toward self-change, rather than changing the
world around him.

—KENNETH KENISTON. "Heads and Seekers: Drugs on
Campus, Counter-Cultures and American Society. *"American Scholar,* Winter 1968–69, Vol. 38, No. 1.

So long as one lives, change is possible; but the longer such
behavior is continued the more force and authority it acquires,
the more it permeates other consonant modes, subordinates other
conflicting modes, changing back becomes steadily more difficult.

—ALLEN WHEELIS. "How People Change." *Commentary,* May
1969

"We are what we do," writes Wheelis. "Action which defines
a man, describes his character, is action which has been repeated over
and over, and so has come in time to be a coherent and relatively independent mode of behavior." At the beginning, the action "may
have been fumbling and uncertain, may have required attention, effort, will . . ." as, for example, the first time one lights up a marijuana cigarette or takes a stand publicly on a controversial issue.

With perseverance such behavior requires "less effort, attention
and begins to function smoothly, and becomes integrated within a

144

larger pattern . . ." But such action "tends to maintain itself, to resist change . . . Often, as in the early stages of drug use when one is experimenting, the realization that one is taking drugs is almost hidden from consciousness until the illusion is cast off. It is at that point that one has to arrive at a conscious decision and to make a choice . . . As to freedom, which means so much to today's youth, Wheelis comments: "Freedom is not an objective attribute of life; alternatives without awareness yield no leeway . . . Freedom is the awareness of alternatives and of the ability to choose . . ." And it is on the freedom to choose alternatives that I wish to conclude this interpretive report of one person's views of the contemporary drug scene that I hope carries meaning for the young.[111]

Young persons, in their justifiable dissatisfaction with the state of our society, may go in either direction. They may yield to a sense of defeatism and cynicism about the possibility of changing conditions, thus rationalizing retreat into privatism and further alienation from the adult world. Or they may decide that this is after all *their* world and may realize that in retreat they are rejecting themselves and their contribution, aside from the fact that they have a very real responsibility to carve out a significant role in changing today's society. There are many adults, working to change the Establishment, equally as concerned as youth about the disastrous drift of our government. They would welcome the energy, the idealism, and passion of the young, and would gladly join with them in a common effort—so urgently needed—to turn us around into a sane and humane society. Ralph Nader has been doing exactly that with young dedicated people who have taken fire from his inspiration, and are turning out searching and valuable studies of how, in fact, our institutions work, too often to the detriment of the common good.

Nader is also working to change the false concept of patriotism that is prevalent today. Patriotism should be a force for making democracy work rather than a "tool manipulated by unscrupulous or cowardly leaders and elites." Conversely, such actions by our government as the war in Vietnam, in particular its continuation despite the wishes of the people, should be considered "unpatriotic" along with the deplorable treatment of returning veterans described in Chapter VIII. As another means of extending the influence of people generally, Nader plans a study of Congress so as to help us make it a more effective instrument for the benefit of people.[112]

The problem areas in which the young are needed makes an extraordinarily long list of which the following are but a few:

• The persistence of hunger amid plenty with subsidies to the big farmers to plough under food. What is preventing ending poverty?

- The persistence of a welfare system that dehumanizes by the failure to provide for a decent standard of living by virtue of the method of caring for those for whom no employment is available.
- The failure of our government to provide meaningful employment for the general welfare rather than for profit. Money now misspent on defense and excessive building of highways should be diverted to the improvement of low and middle-income housing and public transportation.
- The failure in the North as well as in the South to finally end school segregation through opposition to low- and middle-income housing and creation of zoning laws.
- The road blocks that deny the American people a real choice in electing a President, combined with the fact that money available to the candidate rather than qualifications are deciding factors.
- The gross inequalities of our legal system, which fill our prisons with members of our minority groups, particularly blacks.
- The need to make schools even more relevant through joint student-faculty study and conferences, in particular to stop the use of textbooks for the study of current problems that require field work at the sources of the problems.
- The need to include in our elementary and high schools and colleges the teaching of American history as it really was, with the role of all minority groups in true perspective.

The authors of *America, Inc.* have accurately described youth's search for meaning:

> The search of the youth today is for ways and means to make the machine—and the vast bureaucracy of the corporation state and of government that runs the machine—the servant of man.[113]

John Gardner through his organization, "Common Cause," is trying to develop a large, powerful grass-roots people's lobby for creative, deep-reaching change. There is room for the young in local politics. Berkeley, California, the birthplace of campus dissent arising out of opposition to war-related research, now has young radicals on its City Council, which meets to a packed audience of young, interested, and very active citizens. The young have much to contribute in self-help organizations within the ghetto itself, as well as in wider groupings to exert continuous and creative pressure upon city, state, and federal government.

The problems of our society are enormous, but so is the challenge. Here lie true adventure, the possibility for expanding the mind's horizons, the development of a sense of community with like-minded youths and adults, and a real sense of humanity.

Mrs. Coretta Scott King put the challenge to all of us in its true perspective when she said: "For the first time Americans are not smugly content that our system is essentially perfect, and many, especially young people, understandably are questioning premises at the core of the society." She went on:

> If by now the tens of billions so quickly mobilized for war are to be freed we have the first element of a campaign for new life. Well-meaning Americans, black and white, have the task of forcing an end to the war and diverting the billions available, not to Pentagon programs, but to life-giving opportunities.[114]

# For an Understanding of Drug Abuse

"Drug abuse" in this book has been used as the comprehensive term including both addiction and/or dependence. This is so since it is the psychological "addiction" of drug abusers in general that deters them from giving up the habit following a period of detoxification (in the case of physically addictive drugs) or abstinence (in the case of nonaddictive drugs). In this sense, the World Health Organization term *dependence* is useful, if used generally. This is understandable, since many drug abusers, addicts included, are known to have a poor self-concept or image. Building self-confidence takes much longer than the process of detoxification, or recuperation from drug abstinence. Also, the known factors that make individuals *more* susceptible or vulnerable to opiate addiction, in particular, are lacks in the socialization process: lack of stable family life, of education, vocational-professional training, employment and other social lacks found in our urban slums require a much longer period to change if abusers and addicts are to be rehabilitated effectively.

In this book I have used *drug abuse* to mean simply regular use on a continuing basis sufficient to have brought about dependence (physical and/or psychological dependence) that affects social functioning: school work, interpersonal relations, job etc.

A dependence that affects seriously an individual's social functioning is, or should be, of as much concern as the effect on physical functioning since the individual behaves as an integral whole. It is the imbalance in social functioning that brings an individual to the psychiatrist for what we erroneously call "mental illness" as if this were a separate entity from "physical illness."

# Glossary*

*Addiction (drug)*. A state of periodic or chronic intoxication produced by the repeated consumption of a drug (natural or synthetic). It is generally assumed to include: (1) an overpowering desire or need (compulsion) to continue taking the drug and to obtain it by any means; (2) a tendency to increase the dose; (3) a psychic (psychological) and generally a physical dependence on the effects of the drug; (4) detrimental effect on the individual and on society. Because of its combining of compulsion, tolerance, physical dependence, psychological dependence, and detrimental effects, it is not a useful term and should be discarded.

*"Blind."* A term used in research to indicate that the patient or subject does not know what drug is being administered so that any prior expectations of effects of the drug he may have do not influence his response.

*"Double blind."* A term used in research to indicate that neither the patient or subject nor the experimenter knows which of several drugs or placebo is given on any occasion. Considered a necessary condition if results are attributed to the effects of the drug as pharmacologic agent.

*Dependence (drug)*. A state of psychic or physical dependence, or both, on a drug, arising in a person following administration of that drug on a periodic or continuous basis. The characteristics of such a state will vary with the agents involved, and these characteristics should always be made clear by designating the particular type of drug dependence in each specific case.

*Dependence (physical)*. An adaptive state that manifests itself by intense physical disturbances when the administration of the drug is suspended or when its action is affected by the administration of a specific antagonist. Presence of a reliable withdrawal syndrome is considered evidence of physical dependence.

*Dependence (psychic)*. A feeling of satisfaction and a psychic drive that require periodic or continued administration of the drug to produce pleasure or to avoid discomfort; usually does not involve physiological withdrawal symptoms.

*Depressant*. Any agent that will depress (decrease) a body function or nerve activity. Depressants may be classified according to the organ or system upon which they act.

*CNS depressant. Medical:* any agent that will depress the functions of the central nervous system.

*Legal:* a drug that may produce any of the following: (1) calming effect or relief of emotional tension or anxiety; (2) drowsiness, sedation,

149

sleep, stupor, coma, or general anesthesia; (3) increase of pain threshold; (4) mood depression or apathy; disorientation, confusion, or loss
of mental acuity. (Regulations under the Federal Food, Drug & Cosmetic Act, January 1966.)

*Endogenous.* Produced within the cell or the organism.

*Habituation (drug).* A condition resulting from the repeated consumption of a drug. Its characteristics include: (1) a desire (but not a compulsion) to continue taking the drug for the sense of improved well-
being it engenders; (2) little or no tendency to increase the dose;
(3) some degree of psychic dependence on the effect of the drug, but
absence of physical dependence and hence of an abstinence syndrome;
(4) detrimental effects, if any, primarily on the individual.

*"Habit-forming drugs."* Legal: a drug that may produce any of the following: (1) a psychological or physical dependence on the drug (compulsive use); (2) euphoria (exaggerated sense of well-being); (3) personality changes; (4) transient psychosis, deliria, twilight state, or
hallucinoses; (5) chronic brain syndrome; (6) increased tolerance or
a need or desire to increase the drug dosage. (Regulations under Federal Food, Drug & Cosmetic Act, January 1966).

*Hallucinogenic. Medical:* producing hallucinations—false perceptions
having no relation to reality and not accounted for by any external
stimuli; may be visual, olfactory, auditory, etc.

*Legal:* a drug that may produce hallucinations, illusions, delusions, or
alteration of any of the following: (1) orientation with respect to time
or place; (2) consciousness, as evidenced by confused states, dream-
like revivals of past traumatic events or childhood memories; (3) sensory perception, as evidenced by visual illusions, distortion of space
and perspective; (4) motor coordination; (5) mood and affectivity, as
evidenced by anxiety, euphoria, hypomania, ecstasy, autistic withdrawal; (6) ideation, as evidenced by flight of ideas of reference,
impairment of concentration and intelligence; (7) personality, as evidenced by depersonalization and derealization, impairment of conscience and of acquired social and cultural customs. (Regulations under Federal Food, Drug & Cosmetic Act, January 1966).

*Hypnotic.* A drug that induces sleep; usually refers to drugs that induce
normal sleep but may include all narcotics (medical).

*Narcotic. Medical:* a class of drugs that induce sleep and stupor and relieve pain; includes opiates, anesthetics, and others. Some pharmacol-
ogists include barbiturates, although they do not relieve pain.

*Legal:* opium, its alkaloids and derivatives; the coca leaf and its principal derivative, cocaine; the plant *Cannabis sativa L.,** otherwise known
as "marijuana"; and a specific class of synthetics called "opiates" such
as meperidine (Demerol) and methadone.

*Opiate.* A class of drugs having the properties and actions of opium; in-

---

* Marijuana has since been reclassified as a "dangerous" drug, not a narcotic,
by the Federal government but remains to be changed by each state.

cludes opium itself and derivatives of opium as well as synthetic opiate-like drugs not derived from opium.

*Placebo.* "Medication" composed of pharmacologically inactive ingredients (saline solution, lactose, etc.) used as a control in drug research. Used in the same form as the drug for which it is being used as a control (capsule, tablet, solution, etc.).

*Potentiation.* The effect on the body of two drugs, particularly those with sedative properties, which is greater than the sum of the effects of each drug taken alone. One drug intensifies or potentiates the effects of the other. Potentiation may be useful in some cases but dangerous in others.

*Psychedelic.* "Mind-manifesting" or "consciousness-expanding." The term was invented to describe some of the effects of LSD and similar drugs. Refers mostly to same drugs as "psychotomimetics" or "hallucinogens."

*Psychotogenic.* Tending to produce psychosis.

*Psychotomimetic.* A term applied to drugs producing a temporary psychoticlike response.

*Side effect.* A given drug often has many actions on the body. Usually one or two of the more prominent actions will be desired and will be effective in the treatment of a given condition. The other, usually weaker, effects are called side effects. They are not necessarily harmful, but may be annoying. What is a side effect in one instance may be a desirable therapeutic effect in another, depending on the purpose for which the drug is taken.

*Stimulant.* Any agent temporarily increasing functional activity. Stimulants may be classified according to the organ or system on which they act.

*CNS stimulant. Medical:* any agent that temporarily increases the activity of the central nervous system.

*Legal:* a drug that may produce any of the following: (1) extended wakefulness; (2) elation, exhilaration, or euphoria (exaggerated sense of well-being); (3) alleviation of fatigue; (4) insomnia, irritability, or agitation; (5) apprehension or anxiety; (6) flight of ideas, loquacity, hypomania, or transient deliria. (Regulations under Federal Food, Drug & Cosmetic Act, January 1966.)

*Synesthesia.* Subjective sensation of another sense than the one being stimulated, for example, "hearing" colors, "seeing" music.

*Teratogenic.* Producing the development of abnormal structures in an embryo.

*Tolerance.* An adaptive state characterized by diminished response to the same quantity of drug or by the fact that a larger dose is required to produce the same degree of pharmaco-dynamic effect.

*Withdrawal syndrome (or symptoms).* Physiological reactions following abrupt withdrawal of a drug after a period of prolonged and/or excessive use.

# References

1. "Obituary of Walter Vandermeer, Heroin Addict Who Lived to be Thirty in Twelve Years," *The New York Times,* January 12, 1970.
2. "Teenage Use of Heroin Rising But Data Are Few," *The New York Times,* January 12, 1971.
3. *Ibid.*
4. *The New York Times,* February 16, 1970.
5. King, Coretta Scott, "Another Lost Generation of Black Children: Can White Society Find Its Conscience?" Address to American Orthopsychiatric Association, New York City, March 31, 1969.
6. Coles, Robert, Joseph H. Brenner, Dermot Meagher, *"Drugs and Youth,* Liveright Publishing Corp., 1970.
7. N.Y. Academy of Medicine "Drug Addiction III" July, 1965, *New York Academy Bulletin,* Vol. 41, No. 7.
8. Chein, et al, *Road to H.*
9. Winick, Charles, "Drug Addicts Getting Younger," *The PTA Magazine,* Vol. 65, No. 1, September 1970.
10. Otto, Herbert, "New Light on the Human Potential," *Child Education,* Vol. 47, No. 1, September 1970.
11. Bart, Peter, "Advertising: In Quest of Teenage Buyers," *The New York Times,* November 1, 1962.
12. Lennard, Henry L. and Leon J. Epstein, Arnold Bernstein, Donald C. Ransom, *Mystification and Drug Misuse—Hazards in Using Psychoactive Drugs,* Jossey-Bass, Inc., San Francisco, 1971.
13. Parrington, Vernon Louis, *The Beginnings of Critical Realism in America: 1860–1920,* Vol. III of *Main Currents in American Thought,* Harcourt, Brace & World, Inc., New York, 1958.
14. Beard, Charles A., *An Economic Interpretation of the Constitution of the United States.* The Macmillan Company, New York, 1956.
15. Federalist Paper by Madison, *Federalist Papers, The Federal Constitution,* Great Books Foundation, Chicago.
16. Talk to High School Juniors, Dayton, Ohio, 1960, by C. S. Deschin.
17. Lynd, Robert S., *Knowledge for What?,* Princeton University Press, 1948.
18. Brill, Henry, "The Case Against Marijuana," *Journal of School Health,* Vol. XXXVIII, No. 8, October 1968.
19. Coles, Robert, Joseph H. Brenner, Dermot Meagher, *Drugs and Youth,* Liveright Publishing Corporation, New York, 1970.
20. Coles, Robert, "Mix-up on Drugs," *The New Republic,* September 17, 1966.

21. Chein, Isador, et al, *The Road to H, Narcotics, Delinquency, and Social Policy,* Basic Books, Inc., New York, 1964.
22. *The New York Times,* June 17, 1971. Gallup Poll.
23. "Child Health Services and Pediatric Education," Survey quoted in Leona Baumgartner's paper, "Better Health for School-Age Children: A Challenge to Medicine and Education," *The Child,* Vol. XV, August–September 1950.
24. Corson, John J. *The New York Times Magazine,* December 28, 1947. "To Achieve Freedom From Want."
25. "Charity, Behavior and Social Security," *Journal of Higher Education,* Vol. XXI, January 1, 1950.
26. Report of the joint Committee on the economic report of the 81st Congress, "Low-Income Families and Economic Stability," United States Government Printing Office, Washington, D.C., 1949.
27. Cohen, Eli and Louise Kopp, "Youth and Work: The Second Challenge," *Children,* Vol. IX, No. 2, March–April 1962.
28. "Unemployment of Youth: Social Dynamite in Our Large Cities," *Children,* Vol. VIII, No. 5, September–October 1961.
29. *Ibid.*
30. *Ibid.*
31. Packard, Vance, *The Hidden Persuaders,* David McKay Co., Inc., New York, 1957.
32. *The New York Times Magazine,* May 11, 1958.
33. Proceedings of the 38th Annual Conference, Child Study Association, 1962, "Youth in Search of Significance."
34. Wheelis, Allen, *The Quest for Identity,* W. W. Norton, New York, 1960.
35. *Report of the National Advisory Commission on Civil Disorders,* U.S. Government Printing Office, Washington, D.C., March 1968. Supplemental Report: Studies for the National Advisory. . . . U.S. Government Printing Office, July 1968.
36. King, "Another Lost Generation."
37. Wheelis, *Quest for Identity.*
38. Mintz, Morton and Jerry S. Cohen, *America, Inc.—Who Owns and Operates the United States?,* The Dial Press, New York, 1971.
39. Coles, "Mix-up on Drugs."
40. Simon, William and John H. Gagnon, "Children of the Drug Age," *Saturday Review,* September 21, 1968.
41. "Marijuana: Millions of Turned-on Users," *Life,* July 7, 1967.
42. *Ibid.*
43. Simon and Gagnon, "Children of the Drug Age."
44. "The Drug Scene," *The New York Times,* January 11, 1968.
45. *Ibid.,* January 10, 1968.
46. *Ibid.,* January 8, 1968.
47. *Ibid.,* January 9, 1968.
48. *Ibid.,* January 12, 1968.
49. Galdston, Iago, *The Meaning of Social Medicine,* Harvard University Press, Cambridge, 1954.

50. Lennard, Henry L. et al, *Mystification and Drug Misuse—Hazards in Using Psychoactive Drugs.*
51. *Ibid.*
52. *Ibid.*
52a. *Ibid.*
53. Beaconsfield, Peter, "The Other Pollution—Internal—Additives and Drugs Swallowed Carelessly Harm Human Animal," *The New York Times,* January 11, 1971.
54. Taqi, S., *Bulletin on Narcotics,* Vol. XXI, No. 4, "Approbation of Drug Usage in Rock and Roll Music," United Nations, New York, October–December 1969.
55. *The New York Post,* March 6, 1971.
56. Wertham, Fredric, *A Sign for Cain—An Exploration of Human Violence,* The Macmillan Company, New York, 1966.
57. Blum, Sam, "Marijuana Clouds the Generation Gap," *The New York Times Magazine,* August 23, 1970.
58. Nowlis, Helen H., *Drugs on the College Campus,* Doubleday & Company, Inc., Garden City, New York, 1969.
59. Cohen, Sidney, *The Drug Dilemma.*
60. Nowlis, *Drugs on the College Campus.*
61. Keniston, "Heads and Seekers."
62. Cohen, *The Drug Dilemma.*
63. Lindesmith, Alfred R., Ph.D., "Sociology of Addiction," *Illinois Medical Journal,* October 1966, Vol. 130, No. 4, pp. 447–450.
64. Mattick, Hans W., "The Epidemiology of Drug Addiction and Reflections on the Problems and Policy on the U.S. *Illinois Medical Journal,* October 1966, Vol. 130, No. 4.
65. Maryland Drug Abuse Study, 1969, Office of Mental Health, Maryland State Department of Mental Hygiene, David Murco, Principal Investigator and Project Director; Project Officer, Mitchell Balter, NIMH.
66. Mattick, *Illinois Medical Journal.*
67. Chein, et al, *The Road to H.*
68. Brill, Henry, "Misapprehensions about Drug Addiction: Some Origins and Repercussions," *Journal of Comprehensive Psychiatry,* June, 1963, Vol. 4, No. 3.
69. *The Village Voice,* October 28, 1971, "Narcotics Register: One Citizen in Twenty a Junkie."
70. Primm, Beny R., *Medical Opinion and Review,* November 1970, Vol. 6, No. 11.
71. Brill, Henry, *The Journal of School Health,* October 1968, Vol. XXXVIII, No. 8.
72. Nowlis, *Drugs on the College Campus.*
73. *Annals of Internal Medicine,* 1970, Vol. 73.
74. *Ibid.*
75. Kolansky, Harold and William T. Moore, "Effects of Marijuana on Adolescents and Young Adults," *Journal of the American Medical Association,* April, 1971, Vol. 216, No. 3.

76. *Drugs and Drug Abuse Education Newsletter,* April, 1970, Vol. 2, No. 4.
77. Weil, Andrew T., Norman E. Zinberg, Judith M. Nelson, *Science,* December 13, 1968, Vol. 162.
78. Kolansky and Moore, *Journal of American Medical Association.*
79. Zinberg and Weil, "A Scientific Report: The Effects of Marijuana on Human Beings." *New York Times Magazine,* May 11, 1969.
80. Hollister, Leo E. *Science,* April 2, 1971, Vol. 172.
81. Coles, et al.
82. *The New York Times,* May 5, 1970, "Study of LSD Spurs Suspicion of Drug's Link to Birth Defects."
83. Hollister, *Science,* April 2, 1971.
84. *Public Health Notes,* May 1969, The Public Health Association of New York City, May 1969, Vol. II, No. 2.
85. Health Policy Advisory Center Bulletin, June 1970.
86. Primm, *The Village Voice,* June 17, 1971.
87. Health Policy Advisory Center Bulletin (PAC), June 1970.
88. Brill, *Annals of Internal Medicine,* Vol. 67, No. 1, July 1967.
89. Marin, Peter and Allen Y. Cohen, *Understanding Drug Use,* Harper & Row, New York, 1970.
90. Mead, Margaret, *The New York Times,* October 28, 1969.
91. Lindesmith, *The Addict and the Law.*
92. Keniston, "Heads and Seekers."
93. Ingersoll, John, "Drugs and Our Children," a White House Report, *Ladies Home Journal,* May 1970.
94. Farnsworth, Dana L., "The Marijuana Problem," paper presented before American Bar Association, February 29, 1970.
95. Chein, et al, *The Road to H.*
96. Lindesmith, Introduction to "Addiction, Crime or Disease?"
97. New York Academy of Medicine Report on Drug Addiction II, 1963.
98. Straus, Nathan, III, *Addicts and Drug Abusers: Current Approaches to the Problem,* Twayne Publishers, Inc., New York, 1971.
99. New York Academy of Medicine Report, 1963.
100. Simon and Gagnon, "Children of the Drug Age."
101. *The Village Voice,* March 25, 1971, "Legalizing Heroin, the Biggest Bet."
102. *The Village Voice,* October 28, 1971, "Narcotics Register: One Citizen in 20 a Junkie."
103. Mintz and Cohen, *America, Inc.*
104. Lindesmith, *The Addict and the Law.*
105. O'Donnell, Dr. John, "A Post-Hospital Study of Kentucky Addicts, A Preliminary Report," Journal of the Kentucky State Medical Association, July 1963.
106. *The Christian Science Monitor,* June 16, 1970.
107. *UN Bulletin of Narcotics,* January–March 1966.
108. UN Report, November 1969.
109. *UN Bulletin on Narcotics,* July–September, 1971.

110. Mintz and Cohen, *America, Inc.*
111. Wheelis, Allen, "How People Change."
112. Nader, Ralph. *Life,* guest editorial, July 9, 1971.
113. Mintz and Cohen, *America, Inc.*
114. King, "Another Lost Generation."

# Bibliography

## BOOKS

Adams, Nina S. and Alfred W. McCoy (eds), *Laos: War and Revolution* (with an introduction by Noam Chomsky), Harper Colophon Books. Harper & Row, New York, 1970. Especially relevant are the Introduction, Chapters 12, "The Presidential War in Laos," 1966–70; 14, "Air America: Flying the U.S. into Laos," and 15, "Opium and Politics in Laos." The role of opium and heroin in the continuing war and its extension beyond the end of the Vietnam war constitute blocks to early solution to heroin addiction at home.

American Bar Association and American Medical Association, Joint Committee, *Drug Addiction: Crime or Disease?—Interim and Final Reports on Narcotic Drugs,* Indiana University Press, Bloomington, Indiana, 7th printing, 1969. (With an Introduction by Alfred R. Lindesmith.)

Aronson, James, *The Press and the Cold War,* The Bobbs-Merrill Co., Inc. New York, 1970.

Beard, Charles A., *An Economic Interpretation of the Constitution of the United States,* The Macmillan Company, New York, 1956.

Birch, Herbert G., and Joan D. Gussow *Disadvantaged Children: Health, Nutrition, and School Failure,* Harcourt, Brace & World, Inc., New York, 1970.

Bloomquist, E. R., *Marijuana,* Glencoe Press, Division of the Macmillan Company, Beverly Hills, 1968.

Blum, Richard H., and Associates, *Society and Drugs,* Vol. I; *Students and Drugs,* Vol. II, Jossey-Bass, Inc., San Francisco, 1970. 2 volumes.

Chein, Isador, Donald L. Gerard, Robert S. Lee, Eva Rosenfeld, *The Road to H, Narcotics, Delinquency, and Social Policy,* Basic Books, Inc., New York, 1964.

Child Study Association of America, *You, Your Child and Drugs,* The Child Study Press, New York, 1971.

Clark, Ramsey, *Crime in America: Observations on its Nature, Causes, Prevention and Control,* Simon and Schuster, Inc., New York, 1970. (With an Introduction by Tom Wicker.) Particularly Chapters 2, 3, 4, 6 ("Drugs: When Chemistry and Anxiety Meet") and 14.

Cohen, Sidney, *The Drug Dilemma,* McGraw-Hill Book Company, New York, 1969.

Coles, Robert, *Children of Crisis: A Study of Courage and Fear,* Atlantic–Little, Brown, Boston, Mass., 1967. Excellent background for adolescents wishing to find alternatives to drug experimentation and use.

Coles, Robert, Joseph H. Brenner, Dermot Meagher, *Drugs and Youth: Medical, Psychiatric and Legal Facts,* Liveright Publishing Corp., New York, 1970.

Conant, James B., *Slums and Suburbs: A Commentary on Schools in Metropolitan Areas,* McGraw-Hill Book Company, Inc., New York, 1961.

DeQuincey, Thomas, *Confessions of an English Opium Eater and Other Writings,* The New American Library, New York, 1966.

Deschin, Celia S., *The Teenager & VD: A Social Symptom of Our Times,* Richards Rosen Press, Inc., New York, 1969.

Dreiser, Theodore, *An American Tragedy,* The New American Library, New York, 1965. Excellent for understanding how the values of an earlier period have persisted and their corrupting effect as seen in drug abuse and addiction and especially in drug pushing.

Duster, Troy, *The Legislation of Morality,* The Free Press, New York, 1970.

Fort, Joel, *The Pleasure Seekers: The Drug Crisis, Youth and Society,* Grove Press, Inc., New York, 1970.

Frank, Lawrence K., *Society as the Patient: Essays on Culture and Personality.* Rutgers University Press, New Brunswick, N.J., 1948.

Galdston, Iago, *The Meaning of Social Medicine,* Harvard University Press, Cambridge, Mass., 1954.

Glatt, Max M., David J. Pittman, Duff G. Gillespie, Donald R. Hills, *The Drug Scene in Great Britain,* "Journey Into Loneliness," Edward Arnold Publishers, Ltd., London, 1967.

Grinspoon, Lester, *Marijuana Reconsidered,* Harvard University Press, Cambridge, Mass., 1971.

Hentoff, Nat, *A Doctor Among the Addicts,* Grove Press, New York, 1968.

Horman, Richard E. and Allan M. Fox (eds.), *Drug Awareness,* Avon Books, New York, 1970.

Kaplan, John, *Marijuana—The New Prohibition,* The World Publishing Company, New York and Cleveland, 1970.

Keniston, Kenneth, *The Uncommitted: Alienated Youth in American Society,* Dell Publishing Co., Inc., New York, 1965.

————, *Young Radicals: Notes on Committed Youth,* Harcourt, Brace & World, Inc., New York, 1968.

Koen, Ross Y., *The China Lobby in American Politics,* The Macmillan Company, New York, 1960.

Mayor's Committee on Marijuana: *The Marijuana Problem in the City of New York: Sociological, Medical, Psychological and Pharmacological Studies,* Jacques Catell Press, Lancaster, Pa., 1944. (With a Foreword by Mayor F. H. LaGuardia).

Land, Herman W., *What You Can Do About Drugs and Your Child,* Pocket Books, New York, 1971. (With a Foreword by Henry Brill, M.D.)

Laurie, Peter, *Drugs—Medical, Psychological, and Social Facts,* Penguin Books, Ltd., Baltimore, Maryland, 1969.

Lee, Calvin B. T., *The Campus Scene: 1900–1970,* David McKay Co., Inc., New York, 1970.

Lennard, Henry L. and Leon J. Epstein, Arnold Bernstein, Donald C. Ransom, *Mystification and Drug Misuse—Hazards in Using Psychoactive Drugs,* Jossey-Bass, Inc., San Francisco, 1971.

Lindesmith, Alfred R., *The Addict and the Law,* Indiana University Press, Bloomington, Indiana, 1965.

Louria, Donald B., *The Drug Scene,* McGraw-Hill Book Company, New York, 1968.

Lynd, Robert S., *Knowledge for What?,* Princeton University Press, Princeton, N.J., 1948.

MacIver, R. M. (ed.), *Dilemmas of Youth in America Today,* published by the Institute for Religious and Social Studies, distributed by Harper & Brothers, New York, 1961.

Malcolm X., *The Autobiography of Malcolm X,* Grove Press, New York, 1964.

Marin, Peter and Allan Y. Cohen, *Understanding Drug Use: An Adult's Guide to Drugs and the Young,* Harper & Row, New York, 1971.

Mintz, Morton, and Jerry S. Cohen, *America, Inc.—Who Owns and Operates the United States?,* The Dial Press, New York, 1971.

Norman, James, *How to Cure Drug Addicts,* Tom Stacey Ltd., London, 1971. A report of the author's experience as Commissioner of Prisons in Hong Kong, confronted with a heroin addiction comparable, he states, to that of New York in a city a fraction of the size.

Nowlis, Helen H., *Drugs on the College Campus,* Anchor Books, Doubleday & Company, Inc., Garden City, New York, 1969.

Packard, Vance, *The Hidden Persuaders,* David McKay Co., Inc., New York, 1957.

———, *The Waste Makers,* David McKay Co., Inc., New York, 1960.

Parrington, Vernon L., *Main Currents in American Thought, Volume Three, 1860–1920: The Beginnings of Critical Realism in America,* Harcourt, Brace & World, Inc., New York, 1958.

Report of the National Advisory Commission on Civil Disorders, U.S. Government Printing Office, Washington, D.C., March 1, 1968. Supplemental Report: Studies for the National Advisory Commission on Civil Disorders, U.S. Government Printing Office, Washington, D.C., July, 1968. A paperback edition of the Report with a special Introduction by Tom Wicker was published by Bantam Books, Inc., New York, March, 1968, which is described as including the complete text with a notation that this is an advance copy, subject to revision and correction in its official version published by the Government Printing Office.

Schur, Edwin M., *Narcotic Addiction in Britain and America: The Impact of Public Policy,* Indiana University Press, Bloomington, Indiana, 1962. This is considered a definitive study on this subject and corrects many of the myths perpetrated by the Federal Bureau of Narcotics, now the Bureau of Narcotics and Dangerous Drugs, U.S. Department of Justice, and by our press.

Silberman, Charles E., *Crisis in Black and White,* Random House, New York, 1964. Chapters I, IV, and X are especially relevant.

————, *Crisis in the Classroom—The Remaking of American Education,* Random House, New York, 1970.

Solomon, David M. (ed.), *The Marijuana Papers,* The Bobbs-Merrill Company, Inc., Indianapolis, Indiana, 1966 (with an Introduction by Alfred R. Lindesmith and an Appendix that includes the text of the original of the report of LaGuardia's Committee on Marijuana, pp. 277–410.

————, *LSD, The Consciousness Expanding Drug,* G. P. Putnam's Sons, New York, 1968. (With an Introduction by Timothy Leary. An editorial by the psychiatrist Roy Grinker, Sr., presents an objective and scientific point of view, excerpts from which are in the Appendix for Chapter VI.

Straus, Nathan, III, *Addicts and Drug Abusers: Current Approaches to the Problem,* Twayne Publishers, Inc., New York, 1971. (A publication of The Center for New York City Affairs, New School for Social Research.)

Wertham, Fredric, *A Sign for Cain—An Exploration of Human Violence,* The Macmillan Company, New York, 1966.

Wheelis, Allen, *The Quest for Identity,* W. W. Norton, New York, 1960.

### PERIODICALS

Ball, John C. and Richard W. Snarr, "A Test of the Maturation Hypothesis with Respect to Opiate Addiction," *Bulletin on Narcotics,* October–December, 1969, Vol. XXI, No. 4.

Bernstein, Rosalie, "A Profile of Narcotic Addicts on Public Assistance," *Welfarer,* Vol. 11, No. 1, January, 1971.

Binger, Carl, "Living High on Wit, Wisdom, and Love: A life without commitment to others, without dedication to a purpose beyond ourselves, and without a close partnership is only half a life," *Saturday Review,* July 25, 1970.

Blaine, Graham B., "Youth and Today's Environment," *The Journal of School Health,* February, 1970, Vol. XL, No. 2.

————, "The Risk-Taking Behavior of Youth," in Proceedings of American Social Health Association, National Leadership Conference, Nov. 1–2, 1969.

Bland, Hester Beth, "Problems Related to Teaching About Drugs," *The Journal of School Health,* February, 1969, Vol. XXXIX, No. 2.

Blum, Sam, "Marijuana Clouds the Generation Gap," *The New York Times Magazine,* August 23, 1970.

Boehm, George A. W., "Aspirin—It is the Wonder Drug Nobody Understands," *The New York Times Magazine,* September 11, 1966.

Boeko, Jack, et al, "The Drug Problem—Community Center Experience," *Journal of Jewish Communal Service,* 1970, Vol. XLVI, No. 4, Summer.

Brenner, Joseph, "A Free Clinic for Street People: Medical Care Without a Hassle," *The New York Times Magazine,* October 11, 1970.

Brill, Henry, "The Case Against Marijuana," *The Journal of School Health*, October, 1968, Vol. XXXVIII, No. 8.

————, "Misapprehensions About Drug Addiction: Some Origins and Repercussions," *Comprehensive Psychiatry*, June, 1963, Vol. 4, No. 3.

————, "Death and Disability in Drug Addiction and Abuse," *Annals of Internal Medicine*, July, 1967, Vol. 67, No. 1.

Brill, Norman Q. and Evelyn Crumpton, a clinical study on marijuana. *Annals of Internal Medicine*, September 1970, Vol. 73, No. 3.

Brown, William P., "Narcotics Squad, The Golden Arm of the Law, *The Nation*, October 25, 1971.

Browning, Frank, and Banning Garrett, "The New Opium War," *Ramparts*, May 19, 1971.

Carey, James W., and John J. Quirk, "The Mythos of the Electronic Revolution," Part I, *The American Scholar*, Spring 1970, Vol. 39, No. 2; Part II, Summer 1970, Vol. 39, No. 3.

Castelli, Jim, "Vietnam Veterans Wait in Line," *The Nation*, September 6, 1971.

Cheek, Frances E., Stephens Newell, and Milton Joffe, "Deceptions in the Illicit Drug Market," *Science*, February 27, 1970, Vol. 167.

Clark, Ramsey, "Criminal Justice in Times of Turbulence," *Saturday Review*, September 19, 1970.

Cohen, Eli, and Louise Kopp, "Youth and Work: The Second Challenge," *Children*, March–April, 1962, Vol. 9, No. 2.

Cohen, Melvin, Donald F. Klein, "Drug Abuse in a Young Psychiatric Population," *American Journal of Orthopsychiatry*, April, 1970, Vol. 40, No. 3.

Coles, Robert, "Mix-Up on Drugs," *The New Republic*, September 17, 1966.

Conant, James B., "Unemployment of Youth: Social Dynamite in Our Large Cities," *Children*, Vol. 8, No. 5, Sept.–Oct., 1961.

Cook, Fred J., "The Corrupt Society, A Journalist's Guide to the Profit Ethic," *The Nation*, June 1–8, 1963. The entire issue of 44 pages is devoted to an exposé of the lack of ethics of mid-century American society.

Corson, John J., "To Achieve Freedom from Want," *The New York Times Magazine*, December 28, 1947.

Deschin, Celia S., "Child Welfare 1950," *Educational Research Bulletin*, January 17, 1951, Vol. XXX, No. 1.

————, "The Truth Shall Make Us Free," *Adelphi Quarterly*, Summer 1966.

————, "The Future Direction of Social Work: From Concern with Problems to Emphasis on Prevention," *American Journal of Orthopsychiatry*, January 1968, Vol. 38, No. 1.

————, "Knowledge Is Neither Neutral Nor Apolitical," *American Journal of Orthopsychiatry*, April 1971, Vol. 41, No. 3.

Dimock, Hedley G. "Sensitivity Training in Canada: Perspective and Comments," *Canada's Mental Health Supplement*, No. 69, Sept.–Oct., 1971.

Dishotsky, Norman I., William D. Loughman, Robert E. Mogar, Wendell R. Lipscomb, "LSD and Genetic Damage: Is LSD chromosome damaging, carcinogenic, mutagenic, or teratogenic?" *Science,* April 30, 1971, Vol. 172. (See Appendix for Chapter VI.)

Dubos, René, "Man-made Environments," *The Journal of School Health,* September 1971, Vol. XLI, No. 7.

————, "Mere Survival Is not Enough for Man," *Life* editorial, July 24, 1970.

Eisenberg, Leon, "Student Unrest: Sources and Consequences, Changes in adolescence, universities, and society have altered radically the experience of being young," *Science,* March 27, 1970, Vol. 167.

Eisner, Victor, "Alienation of Youth," *The Journal of School Health,* February, 1969, Vol. XXXIX, No. 2.

Ervin, Sam J., Jr., "Executive Privilege: Secrecy in a Free Society," *The Nation,* November 8, 1971.

Fiddle, Seymour, "Some Speculations on Risk Discounting Among Young Ghetto Heroin Users," Proceedings of National Leadership Conference of the American Social Health Association, New York, November 1, 1969.

Gerbunova, Eleonora, "Drug Addiction—How Is It Handled in the USSR?" *Soviet Life,* (Published in English, Washington, D.C.)

Gilbert, Eugene, "Why Today's Teenagers Seem So Different," *Harper's,* November 1959.

Goddard, James L., "Should it [Marijuana] Be Legalized?" *Life,* October 3, 1969.

Goode, Erich, "The Marijuana Market," *Columbia Forum Quarterly,* Winter 1969, Vol. XII, No. 4.

Goulding, Roy, "New Trends in Drug Abuse in Britain," (Principal Medical Office for Drug Addiction, Ministry of Health, London, England). Proceedings of American Social Health Association, Leadership Conference on Drug Dependence and Abuse, November 1967.

Graham, James M., "Amphetamine Politics on Capitol Hill," *Transaction: Social Science and Modern Society,* January, 1972, Vol. 9, No. 3.

Grant, John A., "Drug Education Based on a Knowledge, Attitude, and Experience Study," *The Journal of School Health,* September, 1971, Vol. XLI, No. 7.

Grinspoon, Lester, "Marijuana, The Anxieties of Our Time," *Scientific American,* December 1969.

Grinspoon, Lester, and Norman Zinberg, Criticism in *Drugs and Drug Abuse Education Newsletter,* April 1971, Vol. II, No. 4.

Halleck, Seymour L., "Psychiatric Treatment of the Alienated College Student," *The American Journal of Psychiatry,* November 1967, Vol. 124, No. 5.

Herzog, Elizabeth and Cecelia E. Sudia, "The Generation Gap," *Children,* March–April 1970, Vol. XVII, No. 2.

Hollister, Leo E., "Marijuana in Man: Three Years Later," *Science,* April 2, 1971. Vol. 172.

Keniston, Kenneth, "Social Change and Youth in America," *Daedalus:*

*Journal of the American Academy of Arts and Sciences,* Youth Change and Challenge issue, Winter 1962, Vol. 91, No. 1 of the Academy's Proceedings.

————, "Heads and Seekers: Drugs on Campus, Counter-Culture and American Society," *The American Scholar,* Winter, 1968–69, Vol. 38, No. 1.

————, "You Have to Grow Up in Scarsdale to Know How Bad Things Really Are," *The New York Times Magazine,* April 27, 1969.

————, "Youth: A 'New State of Life,' " *The American Scholar,* Autumn 1970, Vol. 39, No. 4.

————, and Michael Lerner, "The Unholy Alliance Against the Campus," *The New York Times Magazine,* November 8, 1970.

————, "Youth, Change and Violence," *The American Scholar,* Spring 1968, Vol. 37, #2.

Kirkwood, Porter, Jr., "America's Youth Culture: A Revolutionary Potential?" *Freedomways,* Fourth Quarter, 1970, Vol. 10, No. 4.

Kolansky, Harold, and William T. Moore, "Effects of Marijuana on Adolescents and Young Adults," *Journal of the American Medical Association,* April 19, 1971, Vol. 216, No. 3.

Land, Edwin H., "Addiction as a Necessity and Opportunity," *Science,* January 15, 1971, Vol. 271. "Drugs in this concept serve not as an escape *from* one's self but rather as an escape *to* one's self. The use of drugs is a short-cut, which presumably is also a blind alley, for there is no feedback between the product and the integrative process."

Larrimore, G. W., and Brill, Henry, "The British Narcotic System: Report of Study," *New York Journal of Medicine,* 1960, Vol. 60.

Lennard, Henry L., Leon J. Epstein, Arnold Bernstein, Donald C. Ransom, "Hazards Implicit in Prescribing Psychoactive Drugs: Mystification in drug use and models of drug action are reviewed." *Science,* July 31, 1970.

Levine, Abraham S., "Drug Abuse and Alcoholism," *Welfare in Review,* Jan.–Feb. 1971, Vol. 9, No. 1.

Levitt, Louis, "Rehabilitation of Narcotics Addicts Among Lower-class Teenagers," *American Journal of Orthopsychiatry,* January 1968, Vol. 38, No. 1.

Lindesmith, Alfred R., "Sociology of Addiction," *Illinois Medical Journal,* October 1966, Vol. 130, No. 4.

Mattick, Hans W., "The Epidemiology of Drug Addiction and Reflections on the Problem and Policy in the U.S.," *Illinois Medical Journal,* October 1966, Vol. 130, No. 4.

May, Edgar, "Drugs Without Crime: A Report on the British Success with Heroin Addiction," *Harper's,* July 1971.

Merki, Donald J., "What We Need Before Drug Abuse Education," *The Journal of School Health,* November 1969, Vol. XXXIX, No. 9.

Mullin, Laurence S., "Alcohol Education: The School's Responsibility," *Journal of School Health,* Vol. XXXVIII, No. 8. October 1968.

Nader, Ralph, "We need a new kind of patriotism," (Guest Privilege Editorial), *Life,* July 9, 1971.

Nicholi, Armand M., "Harvard Dropouts: Some Psychiatric Findings," *The American Journal of Psychiatry,* November 1967, Vol. 124, No. 5.

O'Donnell, John, "A Post-Hospital Study of Kentucky Addicts, A Preliminary Report," *Journal of Kentucky State Medical Association,* July 1963.

Otto, Herbert A., "New Light on the Human Potential," *Childhood Education,* October 1970, Vol. 47, No. 1.

Packard, Vance, "Resurvey of The Hidden Persuaders," *The New York Times Magazine,* May 11, 1958.

Pearce, Janice, "The Role of Education in Combating Drug Abuse," *Journal of School Health,* February 1971, Vol. XLI, No. 2.

Polner, Murray, "Back From Vietnam; The Sense of Isolation," *The Nation,* September 20, 1971.

Primm, Beny J., "A Methadone Information Brochure," Addiction Research and Treatment Corporation, Brooklyn, New York (no date given).

———, "Report of a Ghetto Addiction Treatment Center," *Medical Opinion and Review,* November 1970, Vol. 6, No. 11.

Pulos, Lee, "The Human Potential Movement: A New Frontier," *Canada's Mental Health,* Special Issue, Sept.–Oct. 1971. Vol. XIX, No. 5.

Randall, Harriet B., "Patterns of Drug Use in School-Age Children," *The Journal of School Health,* June 1970, Vol. XL, No. 6.

Rudner, Seymour, "The Role of Therapy in a Comprehensive Drug Abuse Program," Nassau County Drug Abuse and Addiction Commission, Carle Place, New York, November 1969.

Scott, Jack, "It's Not How You Play the Game, But What Pill You Take," *The New York Times Magazine,* October 17, 1971.

Simon, Samuel A., "GI Addicts: The Catch in Amnesty," *The Nation,* October 4, 1971.

Simon, William and John H. Gagnon, "Children of the Drug Age," *Saturday Review,* September 21, 1968.

Smith, A. Delafield, "Charity, Behavior, and Social Security," *Journal of Higher Education,* January 1, 1950, Vol. XXI.

Smith, Howard K., and Harry Reasoner, transcript of "ABC Round Table on Laos with ABC correspondents in Vietnam: 'You Begin to Suspect that No One Ever Tells the Truth'," April 1, 1971, *The Nation,* April 19, 1971.

Smith, Mickey, Robert L. Mikeal and James N. M. Taylor, "Drugs in the Health Curriculum: A Needed Area," *The Journal of School Health,* May 1969, Vol. XXXIX, No. 5.

Starkey, Lycorgus M., Jr., "A Clergyman Looks at Drug Abuse," *Journal of School Health,* September 1969, Vol. XXXIX, No. 7.

Taqi, S., "Approbation of Drug Usage in Rock and Roll Music," UN *Bulletin on Narcotics,* Oct.–Dec., 1969; Vol. XXI, No. 4.

Toohey, J. V., "Marijuana—The Evidence Begins to Grow," *Journal of School Health,* May 1968, Vol. XXXVIII, No. 5.

Vaughan, Roger, "The Gulf Between Parents and Their Children, *"Life,* November 17, 1967.

West, Louis Jolyon, a study of the chronic use of marijuana and other drugs in the Haight-Ashbury district of San Francisco. *Annals of Internal Medicine,* September 1970, Vol. 73, No. 3.

Wheelis, Allen, "How People Change," *Commentary,* May 1969, Vol. 47, No. 5.

Winick, Charles, "The Drug Addict and His Treatment," *Legal and Criminal Psychology,* Hans Toch (ed.), Holt, Rinehart & Winston, Inc., 1961.

——, "Marijuana Use by Young People," in *Drug Addiction in Youth* (ed. by Ernest Harms), Pergamon Press, New York, 1965.

——, "Drug Addicts Getting Younger," *The PTA Magazine,* September 1970.

Wyant, William K., Jr., "Addiction in Vietnam," *The Nation,* July 5, 1971.

Yolles, Stanley F., "Managing the Mood Changers: Prescription for Drug Abuse Education." *New York University Education Quarterly,* Spring 1971, Vol. II, No. 3.

Zinberg, Norman E., and Andrew T. Weil, "A Scientific Report—The Effects of Marijuana on Human Beings," *The New York Times Magazine,* May 11, 1969.

\* \* \*

*Canada's Mental Health,* Jan.–Feb. 1970, No. 1, Vol. XVIII, "Marijuana and the Law."

*Ladies Home Journal,* May 1970, "Drugs and Our Children," A White House Report.

*Life,* July 7, 1967, "Marijuana: Millions of Turned-on Users."

*Life,* Oct. 31, 1969, "Marijuana and the Law vs 12 million people."

*Life,* Feb. 20, 1970, "Teenagers on Heroin."

*Life,* Feb. 20, 1970, "Life on Two Grams a Day."

*Newsweek,* April 21, 1969, "The Drug Generation: Growing Younger."

*Newsweek,* Sept. 7, 1970, "Marijuana: Is It Time for a Change in Our Laws?"

*Newsweek,* Oct. 6, 1969, "The Troubled American: A Special Report on the White Majority."

REPORTS, PAMPHLETS, PRESS, AND TV

*The Rehabilitation of Drug Addicts,* Report of the Advisory Committee on Drug Dependence, Her Majesty's Stationery Office, London, 1968 (report, 28 pages). (Brought up-to-date in Misuse of Drugs Acts, May 27, 1971). Available only for reference at the British Information Service Library, 845 Third Avenue, New York.

*Cannabis,* Report by the Advisory Committee on Drug Dependence . . . London, 1968 (79 pages).

*Amphetamines, Barbiturates, LSD, and Cannabis: Their Use and Misuse,* Department of Health and Social Security Report No. 124, London, 1970 (75 pages).

Hentoff, Nat, "Youth in Search of Significance," interpretive Report of
   The Child Study Association of America, Inc. Conference, March 12,
   1962, New York.
Proceedings of The Child Study Association of America, Inc. Annual
   Conference: *Where We Are: A Hard Look at Family and Society,* 1970,
   Child Study Association, New York.
Drug Abuse: A Call for Action. Proceedings: National Leadership Con-
   ference on Controlling Drug Abuse, Nov. 12–13, 1967, New York,
   N.Y., American Social Health Association, Social Health Papers, Vol. 3.
The Risk-Taking Behavior of Youth, Report of the National Leadership
   Conference of the American Social Health Association, New York,
   Nov. 1–2, 1969.
New York Academy of Medicine, Committee on Public Health, "Report
   on Drug Addiction," Bulletin of the New York Academy of Medicine,
   August 1955, Vol. 31, No. 8.
New York Academy of Medicine, Committee on Public Health, "Report
   on Drug Addiction II," Bulletin of the New York Academy of Medi-
   cine, Vol. 39, No. 7, July 1963.
New York Academy of Medicine, Committee on Public Health, "Drug
   Addiction III," Bulletin of the New York Academy of Medicine, Vol.
   41, No. 7, July 1965.
*Adolescents; The Quest,* theme of the entire issue of *World Health,* July–
   August 1969.
"Prevention and Treatment of Drug Dependence," *WHO Chronicle,*
   World Health Organization, July 1971.
United Nations Bulletin on Narcotics, Review of the 20th Session of the
   Commission on Narcotic Drugs, Jan.–March 1966, Vol. XVIII, No. 1.
"The Hill Tribes of Thailand and the Place of Opium in Their Socio-
   Economic Setting," UN Bulletin on Narcotics, July–Sept. 1968, Vol.
   XX, No. 3.
UN International Narcotics Control Board (Geneva). Report to the
   Economic and Social Council on the work of the Board, November
   1969.
Report of the International Narcotics Board on its work in 1970. United
   Nations Bulletin on Narcotics, July–Sept. 1971, Vol. XXIII, No. 3.
Higher Education for American Democracy: Report on the President's
   Commission on Higher Education, New York, Harper & Brothers,
   1947, Vol. 1.
Byler, Ruth, Gertrude Lewis, Ruth Totman, *Teach us what we want to
   know*—Report of a survey on health interests, concerns, and problems
   of 5,000 students in selected schools from kindergarten through grade
   twelve. Published for The Connecticut State Board of Education by the
   Mental Health Materials Center, New York, 1969.
*Who Benefits from the American Drug Culture?* Health Policy Advisory
   Center Bulletin, June 1970. The entire issue is devoted to a survey of
   historical and current aspects of today's drug abuse and addiction problems.
Symposium: Curran, Frank J., "Juveniles and Drug Abuse," with illustra-

tive case material and Goldberg, Marion, "Problem of Drug Abuse in Juvenile Court Population," New York State Journal of Medicine, July 1, 1971.

\* \* \*

Blakeslee, Alton, "What You Can Do About Dangerous Drugs," The Associated Press, 1971 (pamphlet, 64 pages).

Calof, Judia, "A Study of Four Voluntary Treatment and Rehabilitation Programs for New York City Narcotic Addicts" Department of Public Affairs, Community Service Society of New York, 1967 (pamphlet, 52 pages).

Houser, Norman W. and Julius B. Richmond, M.D., "Drugs: Facts on Their Use and Abuse," Scott, Foresman and Company, Glenview Alliance, 1969 (pamphlet, 48 pages).

Kurtis, Carol, Drug Abuse as a Business Problem: The Problem Defined with Guidelines for Policy, New York Chamber of Commerce, New York, September 1970 (pamphlet, 64 pages).

Drug Abuse: Escape to Nowhere: A Guide for Educators, Smith, Kline & French Laboratories in cooperation with the National Education Association, 1967.

Ubell, Earl (ed.), The Television Report: "Drugs A to Z," WCBS-TV (pamphlet, 38 pages).

Winick, Charles, and Jacob Goldsteen, The Glue Sniffing Problem, The American Social Health Association, New York (pamphlet, 21 pages).

"Drug Abuse: The Chemical Cop-out," National Association of Blue Shield Plans, New York, April 1969 (pamphlet not paged).

"Drug Abuse—Its Current Status," Symposium presented by The Medical Society of the County of New York, April 22, 1968. New York Medicine, Vol. XXIV, No. 10, October 1968.

Drug Abuse: Game Without Winners: A basic Handbook for Commanders, Armed Forces Information Service, Department of Defense, U.S. Government Printing Office, 1968 (pamphlet, 72 pages).

To Parents/About Drugs, Metropolitan Life Insurance Co., 1970 (pamphlet, 20 pages).

"The Alcoholic American," National Association of Blue Shield Plans, New York, 1970. (pamphlet, not paged)

Someone Close to You Is on Drugs, Addiction Services Agency, Human Resources Administration, City of New York, 1969 (pamphlet not paged).

Answers to the Most Frequently Asked Questions About Drugs, a Federal Source Book, U.S. Government Printing Office, Division of Public Documents, Washington, D.C., 1970 (pamphlet, 29 pages).

Newsday, "Mary Jane Turns on the Profits," Nov. 1, 1970.

New York Post, "A Real War on Drugs?—The Nixon Administration has manifested periodic public concern about narcotics abuse. It might almost be said that its announcements of new control programs were becoming a habit," June 19, 1971.

——— "Addiction Ebbing in Britain," Nov. 11, 1971.

*The Christian Science Monitor,* "We're Dealing with an Epidemic," May 29, 1970, a ten-part series by staff correspondent John Hughes.
—————— "Thailand—'Four-Lane Drug Highway,'" June 16, 1970. "GI's, Narcotics, and Vietnam," June 16, 1970.
—————— "Hong Kong's Thriving Opium Traffic," June 19, 1970.
*The Manchester Guardian,* "U.S. Attacks British Drug 'Surrender'," May 19, 1971.
—————— "Fewer Registered Drug Addicts," Aug. 6, 1971.
*The New York Times,* "The Drug Scene: A National Survey, Jan. 8–12, 1968.
—————— "Meo General Leads Tribesmen in War with Communists in Laos, Oct. 27, 1969.
—————— "Obituary of Walter Vandermeer, Heroin Addict Who Lived to be Thirty in Twelve Years," Jan. 12, 1970.
—————— "Editorial, No One Answer to Drugs," Jan. 19, 1970.
—————— "Editorial, Seeking a Drug Cure," Dec. 25, 1970.
—————— "Study of LSD Spurs Suspicion of Drug's Link to Birth Defect," May 15, 1970.
—————— "Editorial, Subversion by C.I.A.," June 10, 1970.
—————— "Teenage Use of Heroin Rising But Data are Few," Jan. 12, 1970.
—————— "President Orders Wider Drug Fight; Asks $155 Million: Message Opens Addiction Drive; Illinois Aide to Head Special Office," June 18, 1971.
—————— "Drug Use in City Schools," Aug. 28, 1971.
*The Wall Street Journal,* "New Priorities on Drugs," July 7, 1971.
—————— "The Drug Problem Romanticized," Aug. 12, 1971.
CBS-TV Drug Education Program, Moderator, Earl Ubell, Science Editor, Aug. 29, 1970.
NBC-TV, "The 'Legal Pushers'." Aug. 30, 1970.
ABC-TV, Documentary, "Heroes and Heroin," Aug. 21, 1971.

*   *   *

* The above pamphlets have been included to substantiate evidence of the widespread nature of and concern with today's drug abuse and addiction, or dependence.

# *Appendix to Chapter II*

The Constitutional Convention had been a bitter struggle between democracy and the rights of property . . . "In this ceaseless conflict between man and the dollar, between democracy and property, the reasons for persistent triumph of property were sought in the provisions of the organic law, and from a critical study of the Constitution came a discovery that struck home like a submarine torpedo —the discovery that the drift toward plutocracy was not a drift away from the spirit of the Constitution, but an inevitable unfolding from its premises; that instead of having been conceived by the fathers as a democratic instrument, it had been conceived in a spirit designedly hostile to democracy; that it was, in fact, a carefully formulated expression of eighteenth-century property consciousness, erected as a defense against the democratic spirit that had got out of hand during the Revolution, and that the much-praised system of checks and balances was designed and intended for no other end than a check on the political power of the majority—a power acutely feared by the property consciousness of the times."

The "journalistic muckrakers" of the first decade of the twentieth century examined American industrialization "in light of the continental socialism" of the day. "The new ten-cent magazines provided the necessary vehicle of publicity, and enterprising editors were soon increasing their circulations with every issue . . . It was a dramatic discovery and when the corruption of American politics was laid on the threshold of business . . . a tremendous disturbance resulted. . . . It was not pleasant for members of great families to read a cynical history of the origins of their fortunes, or for railway presidents seeking political favors to find on the newsstand a realistic account of the bad scandals that had smirched their roads . . . it was hurtful to business. And so quietly, and as speedily as could be done decently, the movement was brought to a stop by pressure put on the magazines that lent themselves to such harmful disclosures. Vernon Parrington concludes ironically: "Then followed a campaign of education," adding that the substantial result of the movement was the "instruction it afforded in the close kinship between business and politics—a lesson greatly needed by a people long fed on romantic unrealities."

Today, our government rules by deception and lack of accountability. This is manifested in part by attempts to curtail freedom of the press, and the right of dissent. In addition, President Nixon has tried to select for the Supreme Court those who oppose the progressive legislation of past decades, albeit these have not yet been effectively implemented; school desegregation is still more of a casualty than a victory. A few skirmishes in the "War on Poverty" have accomplished little. And we learn that our present government gives little support to efforts to end discrimination. Where is the "Great Society" heralded by President Johnson?

The arena in which action by youth is greatly needed is a large and diverse one. As a people we are stirring. The truth cannot be withheld forever. It is a basic ingredient in making democracy work.

# *Appendix to Chapter III*

Especially significant is John Corson's recognition that these millions "cannot turn to a beneficent free land for the money-wages which alone will obtain essential food, clothing, and shelter." Yet our representatives legislate for these millions as though they "still lived and worked on the farms and in the towns of the early nineteen hundreds." That this was still not recognized in 1971 was the result of a flaw in government and popular concern, and the lack of understanding of the origins of social problems such as poverty and unemployment.

\* \* \*

Owing to the increase in the birth rate after World War II it was estimated that "26 million new young workers would enter the labor force in the 1960's at a time when automation was increasing." In addition, it was expected that about 65 percent of the youngsters living in rural areas where employment is also declining, "will have to move to cities to look for jobs," although they are likely to be less prepared for the kinds of jobs that are available. Although it was recognized that for some, inadequate education and training were obstacles to employment, a major problem was the decreasing rate of jobs for the unskilled, to which "for the skilled" as well needs to be added. In his keynote address at the Mayor's Conference on Youth and Work, A. J. Raskin, labor reporter and editorial writer for *The New York Times* stated that "the harshest impact will fall on the workers who are never hired," who will be our minority groups.

\* \* \*

Conant makes clear that although no one would claim that providing full employment for youth in urban centers "would automatically banish juvenile delinquency . . . ," he suggests that "the correlation between desirable social attitudes . . . and job opportunities is far higher than between the former and housing conditions." He also makes clear that it is largely a Negro problem in the large cities because of discrimination practiced by employers and labor unions.

All the contrary evidence, namely the poor work in school and low scores on tests made by Negroes, is based to a large degree on the performance of children in what are essentially slum conditions. Consequently, I started with the belief that, *given a satisfactory socioeconomic background and educational opportunity, Negro children can be just as successful in academic work as any other group.* Dramatic success has been achieved in more than one instance in raising the aspirations and achievement levels of slum children. [Italics added.]

\*   \*   \*

In view of the close connection in the average person's mind between crime and drugs, the following excerpt from Tom Wicker's Introduction to Ramsey Clark's book, *Crime in America,* is included as background for an understanding of the milieu or social soil in which drug experimentation, use, and abuse occur. Although Wicker cites Clark as the source, it is in essence a condensation, but an accurate representation of Clark's description, which Wicker describes as Clark's "own kind of statistics,"

In every major city in the United States you will find two-thirds of the arrests take place among only two percent of the population. Where is that area in every city? Well, it's in the same place where infant mortality is four times higher than in the city as a whole; where the death rate is 25 percent higher; where life expectancy is ten years shorter; where common communicable diseases with the potential of physical and mental damage are six and eight and ten times more frequent; where alcoholism and drug addiction are prevalent to a degree far transcending that of the rest of the city; where education is poorest—the oldest school buildings, the most crowded and turbulent schoolrooms, the fewest certified teachers, the highest rate of dropouts; where the average formal schooling is four to six years less than for the city as a whole. Sixty percent of the children in Watts in 1965 lived with only one, or neither, of their parents.

This excerpt provides a clear concept of the social roots of drug misuse on the part of so many of the ghetto children and adolescents.

It should be noted that the full text is to be found in Clark's book, Chapter 4, "The Mother of Crime," pages 40–51, and is well worth reading—and in doing so, to the word "crime" should be added: "drug abuse and addiction."

APPENDIX C

# *Appendix to Chapter VI*

In the book, *LSD: The Consciousness Expanding Drug,* David Solomon (ed.), the Introduction by Timothy Leary states: "Let it be said directly that unless you have had a psychedelic experience, great portions of this book will be beyond your present mental categories. If you plan to impose your own rational structure on this book, you will end up with, and within, the limits of your own categories. And that will be everyone's loss."

\* \* \*

In a *New York Times* editorial, "No One Answer to Drugs," published January 19, 1970, it is pointed out that "An undue emphasis on methadone" may divert attention "from the basic need to attack the roots of the drug-abuse problem, which are entwined with the roots of other social problems: housing, education, health care, jobs, family instability, the whole ugly knot of problems which affect so many inner city residents adversely. It may undermine other responses to the drug problem such as psychiatric and other forms of therapy which sometimes rescue addicts from the grip of drugs . . ."

In *"Lysergic Acid Diethylamide: An Editorial,"* by Roy R. Grinker, Sr., M.D. (Chief Editor, *Archives of General Psychiatry,* The American Association), it is pointed out that LSD-25 was introduced as a "psychomimetic drug and became a powerful investigative tool [for research]." It was also used as an adjunct to psychotherapy . . . At this point, the "affective release provided by the drug interested many psychiatrists who administered the drug to themselves, some of whom became enamored with the mystical hallucinatory state, eventually in their mystique" became disqualified as competent investigators. Lay people "bootlegged" the drug for its pleasurable effect, and a few writers published stories and books on the subject for the lay public. Motion picture actors extolled its benefits, and television psychiatrists enacted its curative powers. . . . Here again is the story of evil results from the ill-advised use of a potentially valuable drug, owing to unjustified claims, indiscriminate and premature pub-

173

licity, and lack of proper professional controls. Indeed this editorial is a warning to the psychiatric profession that greater morbidity, and even mortality, is in store for its patients unless controls are developed against the unwise use of LSD-25.

A Progress Report through March 31, 1971—A Five Year Overview by Dr. Gearing of the Columbia Evaluation Unit, notes expansion of the program to include new out-patient units at Beth Israel, Bronx State, the addition of patients from Westchester County and from the New York City Department of Health Methadone Maintenance Program.

The report is general and lacks the kind of identification of the patients, other than ethnic, age and color distribution, the types of employment and related social data other than "the overall decrease in arrests and incarcerations over a three-year period. This, incidentally, is the major impetus—if not the objective of the acceptance of Methadone Maintenance by the authorities and agencies involved in drug treatment. Accordingly, the progress report is focused on evidence of success in decriminalizing heroin "as measured by recorded arrests and incarcerations," which the report indicates "continues to be impressive," and is generally so considered.

From the frame of reference of this book, additional criteria of success should include changes in the patients' social behavior in his everyday life and should lead to eventual freedom from addiction even to a long acting narcotic.

The figures as regards employment are impressive by percentage but involve a small number of men. For example, "of the 48 men who have been in the program at least five years, 37 or 77% were employed." The picture as regards women is also reported as increasing, as the length of time in the program increases. Among the conclusions, it is made clear that

> The results of the New York City Methadone Maintenance Treatment Program continues to demonstrate that *this* program has been successful in the rehabilitation of the majority of the patients who have met their criteria for admission. These results cannot be generalized to the total heroin addict population, nor to other Methadone Treatment programs which may vary in their criteria for admission, the population involved, or the availability of supportive ancillary services.

There is evidence as well of more "supportive" services though these are still inadequately described. It is also reported that the program has reduced the proportion of patients who abuse "amphetamines, barbiturates, cocaine and/or alcohol" which is given as 10% of the patients in the Methadone Maintenance Treatments, but no number is included. It is, however, stated that "a majority of the patients (53%) who demonstrate these mixed addictions have responded well to the supportive services offered, and continue to function adequately with reference to employment and family relations."

A major problem relating to this five-year overview is the fact that patients have entered the program at different periods and under different admission criteria, making it necessary to divide the study population into "cohorts" (groups) of varying numbers, along with the practice of relying on percentages without always indicating the numbers in generalizations. My reservations about Methadone Maintenance Treatment continue and in fact have increased in light of the recommendations of this report concerning research with reference to "the role of Methadone Maintenance in the treatment of young heroin addicts (under 18)."

# *Appendix to Chapter VII*

The *New York Times* of August 17, 1969, reported that the Justice Department was concerned that present contradictory state laws would hinder rather than help federal narcotic and drug laws. Accordingly, the Justice Department was "trying to sell the various states on the idea of a model state drug control act, which would standardize narcotic and drug laws throughout the land and bring them into closer conformity with federal laws."

It would seem to me important for communities to urge their legislatures to adopt such a plan.

# *Appendix to Chapter VIII*

The Weekly Guardian of August 6, 1971 reports for the first time that there is a "drop in the number of registered drug addicts since the big upsurge of drug-taking in the sixties." According to Home Office figures, there were 1,430 registered narcotic drug addicts, 36 fewer than at the same time in 1969). The statistic is described as hopeful. It was noted that:

> An easing-off had been predicted . . . when the increase in regis-
> tered addicts slackened after the introduction of special addiction
> centres in 1968. There was no indication that the drug problem was
> on the decline, but treatment centres had probably contributed to the
> decline in registered addicts. . .

Also noted was the following:

> Of the 1,430 addicts attending treatment centres, the number re-
> ceiving heroin, whether or not combined with other drugs, showed a
> decline. Only 183 received heroin and 992 received methadone, of
> whom 254 were also receiving heroin. The 1969 figures were 204
> (heroin) and 1,011 (methadone) of whom 295 were also receiving
> heroin.

The article includes a statement from the chairman of the British Medical Association's board of science who viewed the "figures with caution." The figures may give a false sense of security.

It is apparent that the British are careful not to overestimate signs of progress in combatting opiate addiction. Subsequently, the Chicago Daily News Service in London confirmed the decrease from 1968 as well as 1969 and added that an important aspect of the decrease is that for the last two years this has been reflected in a decrease in new addicts, though the core of addicts remains but is growing older and fewer through rehabilitation and deaths.

Accordingly, in this author's view, the persistence of our country in a punative approach is inexplicable on any humane or logical basis.

\* \* \*

"The opium trade in Southeast Asia is very much like a submarine that runs submerged most of the time but can be detected by its echoes, . . . and occasionally caught on the surface . . . In April of 1968 the Senate Subcommittee on Foreign Aid Expenditures issued a report that alleged that four or five years earlier, Colonel (who became Vice President) Nguyen Cao Ky, employed at the time by the Central Intelligence Agency, had been active in flying opium from Laos to Saigon. (N.Y. Times, April 19, 1968.) In fact his pharmaceutical ventures took up so much of the colonel's time and energies that the CIA sacked him," deciding that "they could get more for their money elsewhere . . ." In the politics of Laos,* Burma, and Thailand, the influence of opium and the millions of dollars involved in its trade is never very far below the surface . . ."

Publicly, the United States stands four square for the suppression of opium throughout the world . . . There is much talk among official Americans about eliminating opiates at their source: spraying defoliants on the poppy fields; providing support for punitive expeditions—that sort of thing . . . Yet on the subject of the opium trade in Laos there is curious muting of official pronouncements. In U.S. government-sponsored publications on Laos, one is frequently left with the impression that Laos probably exceeds Iceland in opium production, but not by much.

It is widely known that the Central Intelligence Agency supports what must surely be the least clandestine "clandestine army" in the world—the Armée Clandestine of Meo General Vang Pao (N.Y. Times, Oct. 27, 1969). It is less widely known, but still an open secret, that in addition to Laotian Army planes, a number of planes flown by Americans pick up a lot of opium. Most of these are flown by ostensibly civilian pilots working for what one British observer referred to as "your Terry and the Pirates airlines" (Air America; see chapter 14 by Scott in this book). Hill people crossing intoThailand from Laos know about it.

Therefore, it is highly improbable that the U.S. government is totally unaware of the situation.

This brings us to the extent of official U.S. involvement in the trade. There can be little question that the *de facto* policy of Laos is to wink, at the very least, at transportation of opium locally by American quasi-governmental employees. There is further evidence that designated opium shipments are cleared and monitored by the CIA on their way out of the country by air. [Reference here is to the *Christian Science Monitor* of May 29, 1970, which is reported in detail later in the chapter. See also Chapter 6 in this book by McCoy.] If this is true, it reveals a major contradiction of America's stated

---

* From: *Laos: War and Revolution,* Adams and McCoy (eds.), Chapter XV "Opium and Politics in Laos," by David Feingold.

policy on narcotics, as well as a violation of international conventions to which we are a party . . .

\* \* \*

For an understanding of United States—both military and Central Intelligence—activity vis-à-vis drugs in Southeast Asia described in Chapter VIII, it is important to have some background understanding that goes back to the 1950 attacks by Sen. Joseph McCarthy on scholars knowledgeable on China. In the Preface to his book, *The China Lobby in American Politics* (Macmillan, 1960), Ross Y. Koen states:

> United States policy toward China is more deeply involved in domestic politics than any other aspect of American affairs. It was the one area specifically excluded by Senator Vandeberg in 1947 from the scope of bipartisan agreement . . .
> Ultimately, the dissension in Congress over American policy in China led to open questioning of the extent to which the protagonists in the controversy were influenced by the activities of lobbyists and pressure groups. The efforts of the Communists and forces opposed to Chiang Kai-shek have been the subject of many studies and have received wide publicity. The pro-Chiang forces, on the other hand, have received comparatively little attention. Those forces, which came to be known as the China lobby, did, however, arouse concern in Congress and among certain elements of the press during the height of the controversy over China policy. Senator Wayne Morse charged in 1951 that the China lobby was "conducting a violent campaign against American policies in China, chiefly by charging that the State Department, and especially its Far Eastern Division, is a nest of Reds controlled by Communists and fellow travelers."

Koen notes that a year later, Marquis Childs of the *Washington Post* summarized the feelings of many government officials:

> No one who knows anything about the way things work here doubts that a powerful China lobby has brought extraordinary influence to bear on Congress and the Executive. It would be hard to find any parallel in diplomatic history for the agents and diplomatic representatives of a foreign power exerting such pressures—Nationalist China has used the techniques of direct intervention on a scale rarely, if ever seen.

Koen concludes his Preface first by defining the China lobby as including Chinese, paid American agents, business organizations, missionaries, politicians, and many other categories, in addition to Chinese agents of the Kuomintang, adding:

There is, for example, considerable evidence that a number of Chinese officials have engaged in the illegal smuggling of narcotics into the United States with the full knowledge and connivance of the Chinese Nationalist Government. The evidence indicates that several prominent Americans have participated in and profited from these transactions. It indicates further that the narcotics business has been an important factor in the activities and permutations of the China lobby.

To the above, Koen adds: "Such matters can only be fully investigated and exposed, however, by legally established and sanctioned processes. A private scholar or investigator may aid these processes, but his studies can neither set them in motion nor substitute for them."

It is in the interest of eradicating the holocaust that today's drug abuse and addiction are causing to our youth—in particular—that I have gone to the roots of the source—the unbelievable availability of all kinds of drugs, especially the narcotics that command the highest profit—including as well the background essential if we are to restore to our government the ethics of truth and accountability without which the dilemma of the alienation of youth is not likely to be resolved.

## Permissions

Appreciative acknowledgment is made for permission to use material reprinted from the following:

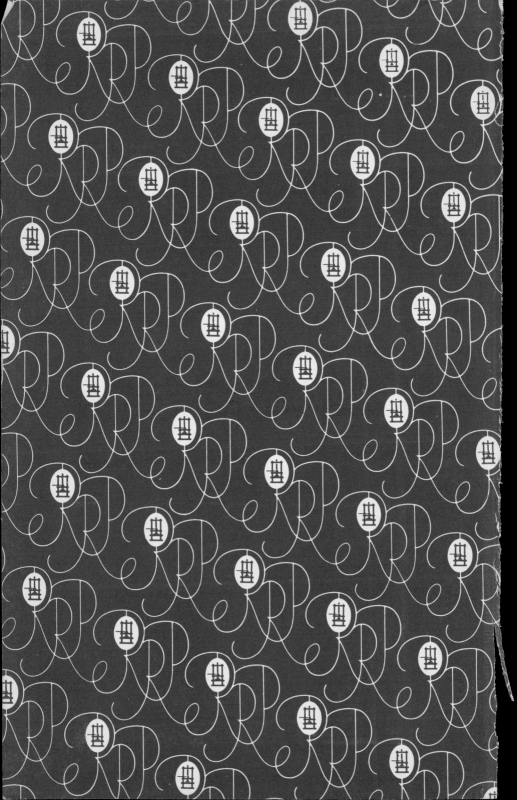